TEEN

is a Four-Letter Word

TEEN

is a Four-Letter Word
A Survival Kit for Parents
Second Edition

Joan Wester Anderson

BETTERWAY PUBLICATIONS, INC.
WHITE HALL, VIRGINIA

Published by Betterway Publications, Inc.
P.O. Box 219
Crozet, VA 22932
(804) 823-5661

Cover design and photograph by Susan Riley
Typography by Park Lane Associates

Library of Congress Cataloging-in-Publication Data

Anderson, Joan Wester.
    Teen is a four-letter word : a survival kit for parents / Joan Wester
Anderson. -- 2nd ed.
        p. cm.
    ISBN 1-55870-156-7 : $6.95
    1. Teenagers--United States. 2. Parenting--United States.
I. Title.
HQ796.A684 1990
649'.125--dc20
                                                    89-29933
                                                    CIP

Printed in the United States of America
0 9 8 7 6 5 4 3 2 1

For Chris, Tim, Bill, and Brian,
who taught me more than I ever
wanted to know about raising teenagers . . .

For Nancy, who promises even more lessons . . .

And a special thanks to the faculty and staff of Arlington High School,
Arlington Heights, Illinois, for their care and interest in this project.

Contents

Introduction

Before I got married, I had six theories about bringing up children. Now I have six children, and no theories.
Lord Rochester, 1947

Once upon a time, you brought a child into your world. Whether natural, adopted or foster, you loved that small creature with an intensity that no one could have described to you, and you vowed to be the best parent the world has ever known. Dedicated and enthusiastic, you researched the merits of strained spinach vs. beets, kissed away the bumps of toddlerhood, answered four thousand daily questions (at least it seemed like that many), and arrived on time for every Parent-Teacher conference.

Remember when you marched little Cindy back to the store to return the candy she'd stolen? When you refused to allow your nine-year-old to lie his way out of that egg-on-the-neighbor's-house episode, and saw to it that he cleaned up the mess? When you wouldn't buy your preteen a ten-speed bike just because "all the other kids have one," and instead suggested that he earn it by getting a paper route? Remember too, all the times when you dropped everything and just *listened*, because that was what your child desperately needed at that moment? The cuddling, hugging and praise generously offered because you knew a child cannot develop happily without tangible expressions of love?

These were all character-building moments for both of you; times when you took the hard road rather than the easy because you knew consistency and follow-through were the keys to your child's well-being. You sensed that love was not the same thing as permissiveness; that real love not only meant acceptance of the child himself, it also included guidance, protection and the occasional setting of limits. It wasn't a snap, and you made plenty of mistakes, but with a combination of luck, instinct and plenty of help from others, you managed. In fact, you managed just fine. And then your beloved child turned into a teenager.

Few aspects of child-rearing terrify a parent more than the dawn of adolescence. After all, we are conditioned to be afraid of it. The media hints darkly of impending drug addiction and out-of-wedlock pregnancy; at the very least, regular sessions with the local youth officer. Insurance companies issue grim warnings about teen-related traffic accidents. We are made painfully aware of the statistics on juvenile runaways, the rising youth crime rate, the number of high-school dropouts. Is it any wonder that we approach these years with trepidation, regarding "adolescence" as synonymous with "delinquency," numbed by the potential for heartbreak, fearful that what we innocently say or do could push our child to the brink of catastrophe?

It is good for us to know that there *are* dangers awaiting our children in the world they must now learn to handle. Years ago, in our primarily rural country, growing up was a relatively simple matter. But today's adolescent finds himself facing a more complex society. Any parent who believes her teen will *not* confront issues such as drugs, alcohol, premarital sex and X-rated films is simply burying her head under a pile of dirty laundry. The changing culture is all around us, and while church and family once could protect teenagers from ominous lifestyles, this is no longer true. That's why it's important for us to inform ourselves, to be aware of the outside influences affecting our teens. Adolescence also forces parents to rethink our own positions on many issues formerly taken for granted. How do we feel about the expressions of sexuality, the use of drugs and alcohol, communication, moral training? What are the absolute "musts" of behavior for our kids, the rules we cannot bend? What aspects can we overlook, realizing that they are annoying but temporary? Unless we adults clarify our own standards and define them firmly—first to ourselves, then to our children—we will vacillate and forfeit our effectiveness.

It is also important to note that even the most loving and caring parents will suffer some rude, wholly unexpected shocks along the way. Adolescence underscores the fact that there are things we simply cannot control. To watch our children making mistakes that could have been prevented is heartbreaking, for when they suffer, we suffer too. Serious problems can and do occur in the very best of families, and sometimes they cannot be anticipated or avoided.

However, we should look at the other side of the coin too. Most teenagers *don't* get into serious difficulties. As a matter of fact, the majority of our nation's adolescents handle these growing-up years with dignity and grace, especially those who come from homes where the character-building groundwork has already been laid. A spate of recent national surveys bears this out, indicating that most young teenagers experience high levels of parental affection and nurturing. In one study, three-quarters of fifth through ninth graders reported that "there's a lot of love in my family"; 65% felt trusted by their parents. It is primarily the troubled, the ill, the traumatized who make it into the headlines and onto the tube. To be sure, there are many of them, but if these poor children were the norm they wouldn't be news, would they?

There *will* be turbulence on the homefront. But these irritations do not necessarily signal the ruin of a teen's life (or yours). What they do indicate are the inevitable stages that every adolescent must experience on his journey to adulthood. And the more we understand these stages, the easier it will be for us to cope with them, and to step in quickly when action is needed.

WHAT STAGES?

More than a generation ago, a book (*Child Development: An Introduction to the Study of Human Growth*, Arnold Gesell and Frances L. Ilg, 1949) for the parents of toddlers outlined a certain behavior pattern in early childhood development, a pattern that every youngster presumably follows. The "terrible two's" (during which a tot balks at discipline and says "no!" to almost everything) are followed by the calmer "three's," a settled-down, relatively peaceful period. By four, bossiness and swagger prevail, only to give way to another burst of pleasant behavior at five. These stages are not exact; that is, not every two-year-old becomes obnoxious precisely on his second birthday—one acts up at eighteen months while another might not become the neighborhood nuisance until age three. Stages vary in intensity and length too; a placid toddler's "no" phase may only last a few months and cause barely a ripple, while a more volatile personality might seem endlessly difficult. If examined closely, however, all toddlers do indeed pass through each of these phases, and each has real meaning and value, providing a solid base for healthy emotional growth.

More recently, in the best-seller *Passages*, author Gail Sheehy defined several stages in adult development, from age twenty through the fifties. Sheehy believes that every adult faces a "passage," a predictable crisis which can result in positive growth, at roughly seven-year intervals. Here again, the phases are not exact in length or intensity, but if one or two are denied or sidestepped, the work of adult growth can be severely hampered.

So it is with your teenager. She too is experiencing predictable phases from the onset of junior high through young adulthood, each "passage" designed to further her quest of "becoming somebody," of determining what the world is like and, ultimately, where she fits into it. Unfortunately for her (and for you), this journey cannot be accomplished smoothly, for it involves tremendous changes in every area of her life.

During adolescence, your child will undergo fundamental and profound *physical* changes, all leading toward the ultimate achievement of sexual maturity. At some unknown and mysterious moment her sexual glands, dormant until now, will send signals throughout her body, activating hormones which begin the maturing process. This growth takes place at an uneven pace, and the adolescent will find herself with an unfamiliar body, difficult to handle in every respect.

At the same time, your teen will be exposed to demanding *intellectual* challenges, all designed to prepare her for a permanent career, one at which she will be expected to excel. Have you glanced at a high school course catalog recently? Most parents can't even pronounce some of the entries, much less understand their content. Pressures will be heavy—grade point average, honor roll, preparation for college entrance exams and concern over developing life goals—at a time when Teen is just starting the physical maturing process.

Your teen must now also make strides in *emotional* growth—the hard work of breaking away from the secure and familiar care of her parents onto a risky, uncharted course. A new way of life must be forged, one that involves the ability to make decisions, accept responsibility, defer gratification, learn the social graces of adulthood, care for her own and others' needs, give and receive love, and develop a personal moral code. The adolescent approaches this task with a mixture of zest and fear, zigzagging across this strange and alien terrain. At times she turns back, comforting herself in the secure warmth of childhood. But ultimately she must press on, driven by an inner need for independence.

Add all these components to a society which often works against the values she is just now trying to establish—and it is no wonder your adolescent is encountering an extremely difficult period of life.

RECOGNIZING TEEN STRESS

Perhaps the subject of stress has been somewhat overplayed in recent years (after all, who *doesn't* experience it from time to time?) but because of all these changes, teens seem to be especially susceptible. And of course, part of their growth involves learning how to handle it. What harms them, however, is becoming overloaded. How can parents tell if this is happening?

Adolescents don't make it easy for adults to help them; their way of showing stress is to be obnoxious, challenging, even rude. But symptoms of stress overload are noticeable anyway, especially if you're attuned to your child's normal behavior (if there is such a thing). First, consider what Teen has been through lately. The death of anyone close to him, a serious, emotional or physical illness (himself or family or close friends), formation of a stepfamily, a breakup with a serious boy/girlfriend, the death of a cherished pet, a move to a new neighborhood and/or school, witnessing a violent event, failing a grade, even a full-time mother returning to work—all of these adjustments and more can take a toll on Teen's well-being. In many areas of the country, just going to school can be stressful; one national survey reported that 40% of teens who responded (many from smaller communities) said that something violent had happened in their schools that year; 22% did not feel safe in their schools. (Ironically, five out of six respondents in this poll favored the use of dogs to sniff out drugs in school lockers.) Is it any wonder kids get overloaded?

Now consider Teen's behavior. Does he have *extremely* low energy (sleeping until noon on Saturdays doesn't count)? Is he excessively worried, indifferent to grades, alone most of the time? Is he experiencing marked changes in eating or sleeping patterns? Most of these warning signs signal an overload of stress. While this condition is usually temporary, it can affect your child's normal passage through the teen stages.

WHAT ABOUT BIRTH ORDER?

Another factor in the way your child goes through his adolescent changes is his order of placement in your family. Although heredity, environment and gender certainly play important roles in making him who he is, recent research is finding that birth order fashions temperament and influences relationships with others to a surprising degree. The "science" of birth order simply proposes that basic behavior patterns seem to occur in most families, and that each child is therefore brought up in somewhat dissimilar ways from one another (but similar to others who share the same family position). Not only do parents treat each child somewhat differently, children themselves tend to handle younger and older siblings in predictable ways, which helps shape the traits associated with each birth order position. For parents, already struggling to cope with the alterations that adolescence brings, understanding the major birth order positions and the typical characteristics that each encompasses can be helpful. For example:

Oldest—We Moms and Dads handle our first baby differently than subsequent tots; we're tenser, more afraid of making a mistake that will somehow ruin her for life, but also an enthusiastic audience for her every accomplishment. Oldest works harder at pleasing us too; she's responsible, self-motivated and legalistic.

When Number Two arrives, a firstborn tries to stay in control by allying herself with adults, and becoming a conformist or "pleaser." Oldests take life pretty seriously, have trouble asking for help, often procrastinate and can be driven crazy by the "little things." Experts tell parents to let up on an oldest, to refuse to reinforce her natural tendency toward perfectionism by improving on everything she says or does. An oldest is usually harder on herself than anyone else could be.

Only—An only child is similar to an oldest in achievement levels, but because he has never been "dethroned" by a younger sibling, he's more self-assured, less competitive or fearful about having to "earn" love or respect. He's also quite content with solitude, ill at ease in the hustle-bustle of a crowded high school, sometimes unsure of how to make and keep friends. Arguing, competing and negotiating can be perplexing for him, and because he probably has more material possessions than peers from larger families, an only may have a hard time sharing. Parents of one tend to be somewhat demanding and overly protective, and probably have more trouble "letting go" as their child matures.

Second—In most families today the second-born is also the youngest, which demographers believe is a pity, because the true Middle Kid tends to be flexible, peace-loving and sociable, thus exerting a leavening influence on society at large. In addition to being the younger of two, a secondborn can also be the next-to-oldest in a large family, or the middle child of three or four (dubbed The Human Sandwich)—thus, her characteristics depend somewhat on the particular structure of her family. In general, however, a younger sibling (whatever the number in her family) tends to "bounce off" the child directly above her, taking on characteristics and interests that will save having to compete with Big Brother or Sis. This can be quite obvious in high school, when a second sister, equally gifted in math or tennis, chooses a different arena in which to shine than did the family's firstborn.

A middle is adept at hiding her feelings, and often believes that no one really cares that much about her. She's less dependent on the family for support, and often goes through more rebellious periods than her older sibling did, forging new ground without searching anxiously for approval. But she does need to feel special, and parents should be sure to attend Middle's high school games or Open Houses (and ask her opinion at family gatherings) with the same interest and vigor they showed the first time around.

Youngest—Whether the second or the last of many, the baby is alternately cherished and teased, thus forming ambivalent feelings about himself. He soon learns to manipulate others, but can remain tied to parental apron strings far longer than appropriate. Charming, carefree and often creative, a youngest's downfall is responsibility—most likely, less is expected of him within the family setting, he tends to underachieve at school and pass the buck in relationships. Parents may well be out of energy by now, but they should push the youngest anyway; the world will not reward him for remaining immature, and he'll benefit from structure and consistency.

No theory covers all contingencies, but understanding birth order traits is one more tool in the arsenal of parental wisdom.

THE ADOPTED CHILD

If your child is adopted, this factor adds an extra dimension to his teen journey. For although it's relatively easy to satisfy the curiosity of a younger adoptee, by the time a child reaches puberty, he needs the story retold more fully. Since the adolescent's job is to separate from his parents and develop his own identity, the adoptee needs to go through this process, **as** well as he can, with *two* sets of parents.

For an adopted adolescent, this essential sense of personal identity can be clouded because there's a history connected with him that he knows nothing about. Kids can get the idea that parts of them are actually missing—how much of their heritage is biological, for example, and how much is tied to their adoptive environment? Where did they get their love for music, their aptitude in science? Teens report wondering why they were given away, whether their natural parents think of them on their birthdays, whether they've inherited illnesses or have natural siblings. "When my friends ask me about it, I sometimes feel like a freak," one sixteen-year-old admits. "Sometimes I wish they didn't know."

Experts agree that a teen adoptee has a right to know some basic facts about who his birth order parents were, even though he may never express a desire to seek them out. Solving the mystery of his origin is usually difficult, however, because most states still uphold sealed files. Despite lack of solid knowledge, adoptive parents can do much to help their teen come to terms with some of these questions.

Although you may feel somewhat threatened by your teen's new interest in his background, try to be as open as you can about the subject. Romanticizing the event—"you were a special child chosen just for us"—is nice, but at this point, your adolescent needs more. Talk to him about the kind of courage it took for his biological mother to give him up; explain why his fears about being "illegitimate" are not relevant ("illegitimacy" means "not legal," and any child who is adopted is "legal"; being born out of wedlock has no stigma at all today, and never did determine the worthiness of any individual); give him whatever rudimentary information you can about his past. It's healthy to admit to Teen (if it's true) that his questions make you uneasy, as if you didn't fulfill all his needs, or that you will be compared unfavorably with his birth parents someday. You may be surprised to discover that, in most cases, a curious teen feels neither different or disadvantaged, but is simply following the same fundamental instinct that others his age have: to learn as much as he can about himself and where he fits.

WHERE DO WE START?

Given all these caveats, most parents ask two basic questions about rearing teens: what are these fundamental stages of growth, and how do we handle them? Throughout this book we will be examining each stage in detail (always remembering that they do not occur on a precise timetable). Such examination can provide added insight, and deepen our understanding of what that uncommunicative fifteen-year-old hulk is actually experiencing right now. On these pages you'll find the reassurance and guidance that other parents and friends have willingly contributed. Formal support groups also will be suggested, as needed. There is a lot of help available today, and there is no disgrace in taking advantage of it. By sharing and struggling together, we increase our own expertise, and become more confident in this most important role. How do you handle your teen? Here are some suggestions that may help:

1. Give your teen firm guidelines. This is probably the most important thing you can do for her. The adolescent must transfer authority from parent to herself, but this is a gradual process, one that works best within an orderly framework. Obedience to reasonable demands can and should be expected; in fact, the presence of external norms and limits symbolize to teens that they are wanted and loved. Adolescents get nervous and anxious when this orderly framework is missing; they may even act out their anxiety in forms of rebellious behavior. It's as if they're saying, "I'll make you notice me! I'll make you care!"

Parents also have a decisive role to play in providing a good environment, for this factor greatly influences the maturing process. Home should be a safe, secure refuge, a place where your teenager can relax and be herself (however irritating that "self" may sometimes be). And parents must be steady and strong, a balance to the teenager's inconsistency. Adults who abdicate their position of authority too early, allowing their teenager to slip into situations he can't handle, may produce an offspring who overreaches his boundaries and comes to grief. On the other hand, parents who refuse to acknowledge his or her emerging need for independence, who arbitrarily hold back the growth process, may end up with a rebellion on their hands, a child who will quarrel over *anything*, just to assert his worth.

2. Live up to your principles. We adults must also remember that our youngsters are now at an age when blind hero-worship of Mom and Dad has ended. While secretly they want to be like us, and desperately need our approval, they no longer accept the "do as I say, not as I do" theory. (Actually, they never did, but at this stage they're more apt to tell us about it!) Therefore, the standards we set must be more than just verbal commands; instead we must master the same behavior we expect from our offspring. An alcoholic mother, for instance, has no right to demand that her daughter refrain from using drugs. Parents who engage in constant violent outbursts cannot expect teens to control their own tempers. A father who shares lewd jokes or X-rated movies with his son shouldn't be surprised if

the boy's sexual values go out of kilter. Teens, seeking to form their own standards, are especially sensitive to hypocrisy in their role models. "Why should we live according to rules our elders break?" they ask. It's a good question, isn't it?

3. Are you looking forward to your children's teen years, or dreading them? If you expect difficulty with your teen, you will probably get it. Sociologists feel that your attitude can be a self-fulfilling prophecy. But if you can trust until you are given reason *not* to trust, emphasize the positive qualities in your child and express faith in his innate goodness and wisdom, he will often go to heroic lengths to live *up* to your opinion of him.

Despite his weird clothes, newfound personality quirks and strange habits, the adolescent is a person too. What frightens him are the same things that frighten every member of the human family—loneliness, feelings of inadequacy, insecurity hidden behind a brave front, problems with family and friends, confusion and concern about the future. Am I lovable? Am I worthwhile? Do I have something to contribute? Who among us does not continue to deal with these issues every day? To the uneven teen, such problems are magnified out of proportion. But if parents can acknowledge his feelings and treat him with respect, tensions can be lessened.

Parenting teenagers is a juggling act worthy of any circus. But the experience can be fascinating too, and full of wonder. These people we are raising have not suddenly turned into alien beings. They are going through difficult times, yes, but they want to be a part of our lives as they have always been, to communicate with us, to understand and to be understood. They long to be challenged, acknowledged, valued. They can handle the word "no," in fact, they may welcome it and respect us the more because we care enough to use it. Most of all, our teens still love and need us very much.

We, in turn, have a valuable and exciting role to play in this, their final stage of life in our care. To turn away because the task is too difficult, to regard our kids as saints, sinners or just plain nuisances, is to miss out on something wonderful, an experience that, with this particular child, will never come again.

It's not going to be easy. But we've come too far to miss the end of the journey.

Chapter 1

Junior High:
The Inconsistent Years

Mother Nature is providential. She gives us twelve years to develop a love for our children before turning them into teenagers.
William A. Galvin, 1960

"Oh Mother, you just don't understand!" "But all the guys are wearing them!" "Don't you *dare* look at me in that tone of voice!"

So dawns the beginning of adolescence, the junior high years. School systems segregate this age group. Society barely tolerates them. Parents are perplexed, uncertain, often annoyed. "What has happened to Sue? She used to be such a nice child ..."

Well, a "child" is exactly what Sue used to be. She lived in a carefree world then, safe and enclosed in the cocoon of her parents' love. She adored Mommy and Daddy. Though she occasionally tested their authority, she knew without question that they were perfect in every way. School was sometimes a bore, but unless she was having extreme learning problems, Sue accepted academics goodnaturedly. The classroom was an inevitable part of life, and she knew precisely where she fit. Socially, Sue's tastes were democratic. She could play as easily with a six-year-old neighbor boy as with the girls from her scout troop, conduct an interesting conversation with the grocer or Grandma. It was all part of that free-spirited, trusting, and secure atmosphere called "childhood."

But as Scripture reminds us, "When I was a child, I used to talk like a child, think like a child, reason like a child. But when I became an adult, I put childish ways aside." Stirred by the mysterious inner prompting of nature, Sue is now beginning to "put childish ways aside." Nothing unusual has "happened" to her; instead she is simply setting forth on her journey to adulthood. This road is never traveled smoothly, but it becomes even more complicated when we realize that no two children are going to travel it at exactly the same pace. And this observation brings us to the hallmark of the junior high age: inconsistency.

THE RANGE OF MATURITY

"The range of maturity in junior high is just astounding," says one seventh-grade teacher. "In the same class I can have a girl still interested in playing with dolls, someone who is literally a child, who hasn't begun the maturing process. And across the aisle will be another twelve-year-old girl; this one curvy, filling out a bra, and very aware of herself as a provocative creature."

Added to the confusion is the fact that physical and emotional growth do not usually coincide. "That tall muscular eighth-grade boy is just a child inside," this teacher explains. "Because of his looks, society raises its expectation of him. And yet he's certainly not capable of acting as an adult just because he resembles one."

"We call them the 'in-betweeners,'" adds a school principal. "Too young to be sophisticated, too old to be cute. And there are no 'average' junior high students. Each one, because of his or her rate of physical and emotional growth, is very much an individual."

Because each child progresses at his or her own pace, there is no "magic moment" when the dawn of adolescence can be pinpointed. Nor is it heralded by a bolt of lightning or other unmistakable signs. Instead, puberty comes on sneaky feet, bringing small changes barely noticed at first.

"I guess our initial clue was when Bobby grew a bit silent," one mother reminisces. "He had been talkative, enjoyed family discussions and always asked a lot of questions. At twelve or thirteen, he retreated—not all the time, of course, but often enough to make us notice."

"My daughter's personality hadn't undergone any evident changes," another parent recalls. "But one morning as we were chatting, I looked at her and noticed the slight but unmistakable rounding of her breasts under her T-shirt. I remember thinking, 'It can't be—she's just a child!' But that was the beginning."

SEXUAL PREPARATION

While puberty involves all kinds of growth, physical transformations are the most obvious. And it's important that kids be prepared for these changes long before they occur. Preteens need to be told what's going to happen to their bodies and why, and they also need reassurance that such a metamorphosis is normal and quite wonderful. Although we parents are sometimes hesitant about imparting sex information because of our own awkwardness or feelings of inadequacy, it's important that we cover the subject before our children reach junior high age. Preteens can accept the news with detached interest and little or no embarrassment. After all, it's not happening to them yet, so there's no personal involvement. And by the time our kids are twelve or thirteen, they're not interested in talking to us about much of *anything*, and our most fruitful opportunities have been lost.

There are many ways to approach the subject. Good books can help, and a parent can always begin by saying, "I suppose you've been wondering about ... " (Just watch even the most casual youngster's eyes light up at this approach—he definitely *has* been wondering!) Keep paper and pencil handy to draw a diagram or two for the more scientifically minded boy or girl, and if you don't know the answer to a question, don't be afraid to say, "That's a good question—I'll find the answer and let you know." Most important is the attitude you convey. This is a natural but very special part of life, a gift that your child will someday use wisely and well. For the present, as questions come up, communicate that you stand ready to help in any way you can. Seeing your child grow and develop into adulthood is making you a very proud parent.

Note the positive emphasis. It's not necessary to convey a lot of "don't's" to your child; instead, you wish to make him feel secure and confident with his emerging sexuality, and to keep the lines of communication open. Sex-related matters will surface again and again during adolescence, and to give proper guidance, you've got to lay a foundation of candidness and trust.

PHYSICAL CHANGES IN GIRLS

If your daughter is "average" (always remembering that there is no such child!), junior high will be her most rapid period of growth. Menstruation begins, although her cycle will be irregular at first. Her breasts start to enlarge, underarm and pubic hair appears, and by eighth grade graduation she will have achieved about 90% of her adult height. Some girls feel sensitive about their menstrual periods initially, asking Mom not to tell Dad or anyone else about it and absolutely refusing to purchase their own supplies. But most accept the inevitable as positive evidence of maturity. Some more eager types demand bras or razors long before there is any apparent need, but in this case, wise parents give in. Acknowledging that your little girl is becoming a woman does wonders for her shaky self-esteem. She isn't at all sure that the miracle will *ever* occur.

And while it isn't necessary to post a notice on the family bulletin board announcing that Miss Eighth-Grader is having her period, it also isn't prudent to play elaborate games in order to hide the fact, as if it were something to be ashamed of. Menstruation is as much a natural part of life for women as breathing and eating, and families do both daughters and sons a real disservice if they portray a hush-hush attitude about it. One of the easiest ways for boys to understand and accept the physiological makeup of women is through experience with their sisters' growth. Such understanding helps them become more confident about their own sexuality, too. So if evidence of menstruation is noticed by a brother, it's fine to say, "Yes, Janey is having her period right now," or even encourage Janey to do the talking. The fewer unnecessary mysteries between the sexes, the more open future relationships can be. Male teasing should never be tolerated.

Junior high girls are quite critical of their bodies. Their hair is too curly or too straight, their thighs gross, their noses absolutely deformed. Despite this apparent repugnance, they can spend hours in a locked bathroom, gazing into the mirror while frustrated family members pound on the door. What your daughter is doing, of course, is getting acquainted with her new image in every detail, though it's hard to explain that to a father who's going to be late for work unless he can shave—*now*! Parental patience is essential at this stage. If you have two bathrooms, count your blessings.

Most girls eventually come to terms with their looks, feeling somewhat comfortable with the women they are becoming, but this will probably *not* happen during junior high. If your daughter absolutely refuses to acknowledge these changes, however—avoiding a bra; feeling not just uncertain but *angry* about her menstrual period; showing no interest in makeup experimentation or clothes—you'll want to delve a little deeper. It's possible that she's a bit fearful about growing up and needs reassurance that it's a normal thing to do. If you aren't able to reassure her, does she have an older sister, a trusted aunt, a teacher, or a family friend to whom she can talk?

ANOREXIA NERVOSA AND BULIMIA

Another physical change experienced by most preteen girls is weight gain, triggered by the metabolic changes taking place within her. Unfortunately, our culture puts a great deal of approval on thinness (and the apparent control needed to be thin); according to one recent poll, over 30% of twelve- and thirteen-year-old girls think they are overweight, and are always on a diet. The number jumps to 40% at age fifteen. While it is true that obesity is increasing in our country—and children are making more and more of their own eating decisions, due to working parents and the microwave food industry—many girls are afraid to eat at the very time when their bodies most need good nutritious food.

Typically, your daughter may try fad diets—one week it's lettuce, the next bananas—but most are short-lived and ineffective. Girls also have a tendency to skip breakfast; it's an unfortunate habit, but there's not much you can do, short of occasionally whipping up something frothy and nutritious in the blender. The situation becomes serious, however, when an eating disorder develops. The two kinds of eating disorders most often recognized are anorexia and bulimia. An anorexic (whose average age is sixteen and who can begin as early as nine or ten) usually starts innocently, simply wanting to lose a few pounds. Instead, she becomes so preoccupied with the control factor in dieting, that she loses sight of what is a proper weight for her and becomes obsessed with the whole subject of food. Ironically, most victims of eating disorders are of normal or almost-normal weight.

Anorexics literally starve themselves, cutting back at first, perhaps, by eating only fruits and vegetables, then moving to unrealistically tiny portions. It is not uncommon for an anorexic to step up physical exercise at the same time she is starving herself, perhaps working out to exercise tapes or in a gym three or four hours a day. She may develop bizarre food rituals or dress in extremely baggy clothes. As she continues to lose weight, she can experience fainting spells, hyperactivity, cessation of menstruation, brittleness and loss of hair as well as irritability and growing disinterest in school. In extreme cases, an anorexic can starve herself to death.

Bulimia, also called the binge-purge disease, starts at a later age, perhaps triggered by a significant life change such as going away to college; it sometimes follows a period of intense dieting. Bulimics don't starve themselves; instead, they consume a massive amount of food, sometimes as much as 20,000 calories at a sitting, then force themselves to throw everything up so they won't gain weight. This ritual may occur several times a day, along with frequent use of laxatives to further purge themselves.

Bulimia has as many dangerous side effects as anorexia because vomiting does more than rid the body of food. It can interfere with how the heart works, damage the esophagus, ruin teeth and gums by wearing away the enamel and also make salivary glands swell, resulting in a "chipmunk cheek" look. Bulimics are harder to spot than anorexics because they show no apparent weight loss, but regular trips to the bathroom after meals can be a sign, along with constantly empty kitchen cabinets.

What triggers an eating disorder? Since so many teenage girls are concerned about their weight, why do some become sick and others don't? While recent research indicates that some cases may be hormone-linked, the most popular theory states that victims of these diseases tend to be "good little girls," showing a long pattern of perfectionism and high achievement in grade school, and an extraordinary need to please parents at home. When these girls reach adolescence, they're reluctant to forfeit their "goodness" image or rebel openly; instead, they assert control over themselves—and their helpless parents—by refusing to eat.

The vast majority of anorexics are females; males seem to avoid the syndrome because they seem less subject to mood disorders, and less concerned about body image. But, interestingly, males who run excessively have many of the same personality characteristics as female anorexics—they are perfectionists and do not express feelings easily—and can become obsessed with running in the same way that their female counterparts are obsessed with food. An occasional high school wrestler, or those in other weight-related sports, also slips into bulimia by making himself vomit in order to stay within a certain weight range. Fortunately, recent research shows that eating disorders occur less frequently than was once assumed. It's now estimated that between two and five percent of women between the ages of fifteen and thirty are afflicted, and a far tinier percentage of men. Professional treatment of eating disorders is essential, and the earlier the better. Possibilities range from hospitalization to therapy to anti-depressant drugs to self-help groups, but should encompass a wide range of treatments because, since an eating disorder may have nothing to do with food, other issues may also need to be addressed.

PHYSICAL CHANGES IN BOYS

As girls undergo their junior high growth, they leave their male classmates far behind. Only a handful of boys will develop dramatically during late grammar school; in fact, some tend to get rather chubby for a few years, which is devastating, even if they know it's only temporary. Genital size may start to increase, and a few boys will experience an occasional erection or nighttime ejaculation. These episodes can be very upsetting to a boy, especially since they occur without warning. It's a rare young man who's going to broach the subject with Mom or Dad. A wise parent calmly acknowledges that this situation is occurring, or will occur quite soon, reassures Son that it is perfectly normal, and matter of factly suggests that wearing an athletic supporter all the time might make him feel more comfortable. You can also show him where the clean sheets are kept. Your son probably won't meet your eyes during this discussion, much less respond to it, but he will be grateful for your understanding comments.

Although most boys don't develop much during this period, their vocal chords start to thicken, producing deeper voices. The same thing happens to girls, but the result isn't as obvious. This can be an embarrassing transition for your son; one moment his voice is in the bass range, then inexplicably it slides up into a hoarse falsetto. This may be one reason why a boy "clams up" at this point—who knows what sounds will emerge if he does try to make a point? It helps if parent ignore the episodes; the thirteen-year-old is going to take enough teasing about it from his classmates or younger siblings.

Most boys also discover cleanliness in the junior high years. While previously he had to be dragged to the bathtub, undergoing lectures about the purpose of soap and washcloths, a boy now cannot pass the bathroom without stopping in to take a shower. Shampoo consumption increases dramatically. His need for constant cleaning is apparently all tied into his emerging body image. He wants to do something to make himself attractive, even if only hygienically.

To fuel his rapidly growing body, a boy develops a voracious appetite. Now you're witnessing the start of the "bottomless pit" syndrome; boys can literally make a career out of eating right up until they leave for college. (Then, thank goodness, it's the school's problem.) It's not at all unusual for a boy to arrive home from school in a state of utter starvation, devour three or four sandwiches while anxiously asking "What's for dinner?" at five-minute intervals, consume a feast fit for a longshoreman at six p.m., and be found foraging in the refrigerator an hour later, to see if anything has grown there since his last inspection.

Both boys and girls of this age need snacking choices that are especially nutritious. They'll get enough empty calories at the local fast food establishment. Try to stock plenty of raw fruits and vegetables, cheese, and nuts for quick pick-me-ups. Homepopped corn offers food value, too. If your teen is a big milk drinker, cut your mounting dairy bill by mixing a few quarts of powdered milk each evening and adding it to the real stuff. He'll never notice by morning.

CHANGING RELATIONSHIPS WITH PARENTS

The hallmark of the junior high teenager is inconsistency; and nowhere is it more evident than in his relationship with his parents. Remember, the work of the adolescent is to draw away from the secure bastion of home and family and to establish himself as a person in his own right. He cannot sever this connection in one swoop, however, because the shock would be too great, the risk too overwhelming. Instead, he initiates this shift in small ways, by denying the importance of his parents, and sometimes becoming very critical of them.

During these "down" episodes, mothers take a lot of heat, especially from daughters. Mom's clothes are relics from the covered wagon days, her hairstyle pathetic, her attitude feudal and her mere existence a problem. If she has the nerve to appear at school (if only to deliver Daughter's forgotten lunch), Daughter is mortified for days afterwards (although she will condescend to eat the lunch). Those cozy mother-daughter sessions baking cookies or shopping for clothes have given way to Daughter racing up the stairs, slamming the door and shouting, "Oh Motherr-r, you just don't understand!"

Oddly enough Daddy sometimes does. Some girls, but by no means all, draw a bit closer to their fathers during this time, perhaps as compensation for having to cast off the feminine role model. Often Dad can get across points that would be rejected if they came from *her*.

But Dad catches his lumps too, if there is an adolescent male in residence. While less vocally dramatic, a junior high son now scorns his father's overtures. What if the guys saw him bowling with *Dad*? Son is in a state of chronic humiliation over his father's jogging outfit, golf score, and TV preferences. However, he will accept money from Dad, and car rides too, as long as the chauffeur remains mute. And of course Dad should be part of the audience at concerts, sporting events, and other places where Son performs. But Dad shouldn't expect to talk to him afterwards, and will have to return home alone.

While a boy will occasionally yell and carry on, his favorite defensive weapon is a startling reticence around the house. "Who, me?" and "Pass the ketchup" are about as chatty as he gets.

Of course, not all generalizations about the teenage years will apply to your teenager. Some kids make very few waves at home; others apparently like to stir things up at every opportunity. Sometimes criticism is not directed *at* parents, but only spoken *about* them. "Most of my friends like their parents a lot," confided one boy, "but we all complain about them anyway. It's sort of the 'cool' thing to do."

Junior high offspring spend a lot of time in their rooms, usually behind locked doors, wondering why their parents don't understand them. And yet they give us little to go on, few chatty intimate revelations which could make the muddle clearer for everyone. When they *do* talk, it tends to come in an unexpected rush, a sort of hurrying to get everything said before the next secretive mood descends. And even during these rare moments, few personal thought are revealed.

Although this behavior is normal for the junior high set, it's still hard for parents to take. It's as if we have somehow, almost overnight, turned into the Enemy. And yet our obligations continue. The most vital one at this stage is consistency, to balance our children's up-and-down moods.

"I see parents yelling their heads off about a broken rule one week, and the next week letting the same thing slip by without a murmur," says a youth counselor. "It's the worst way to handle a junior high student, because the parent must be stable. He's the one who has to remind the zig-zagger that he or she lives in a world where order, rules and expectations abide. The kids need something firm, something that doesn't change even though everything else in their lives is topsy-turvy." In short, structure gives our kids a secure base from which they can safely explore and experiment.

How does this consistency or structure manifest itself?

1. Set only a few rules, and then be sure they're taken seriously. Your teenager should know precisely what is expected of him at home, in the way of chores and basic behavior. Remember, he'll test you at every turn. He's trying to convince himself that he can live very well without you. So you have to make sure that you'll have the stamina to back up the demands you do make. Think about what is really important in your child's character development. Ask yourself, "Will this problem really matter in ten years' time? Is it important enough to make it a burning issue in our household?" If the answer is no, then don't waste your energy on it. There are plenty of issues that *do* matter, and you don't want to give your attention to minor irritations at the expense of major developments.

2. Be available. With the advent of single-parent families and/or double wage-earners, time is at a premium in many households. Yet it's crucial that your offspring feel they can come to you whenever they choose (and they're liable to choose some very peculiar moments). Few things hurt a youngster more than being pushed aside when he has something vital to share. It's as if a parent is saying, "You don't matter—your feelings don't interest me. I have more important things to do." A busy parent doesn't mean to convey this, but the overly sensitive junior high schooler will often take it in this spirit.

Instead, create opportunities for your junior high person to express his concerns and talk freely about them (sometimes just getting things out in the open helps him to cope better). Make sure that he knows that you are interested in talking with him, that you will try not to pry but, because you love him you will want to touch base with him regularly. On those rare occasions when he does open up, really listen. Watch his face intently, smile, ask a follow-up question, let him know that you are glad he is sharing this moment with you. Much young teen conversation is total tedium—"And then he goes . . . and then I go . . . and then he goes . . ."—but if you are bored, try to hide it. Some kids have to babble a bit and test the waters before seizing hold of the real issue. Superficial conversations do offer a benefit, however; alert parents get a handle on what's happening among their children's pals, which teachers are "cool," what fads are definitely in or out. Believe it or not, such knowledge can be valuable—contemporary youth culture is fast-paced and adults often misinterpret it.

Remember, the child who can chat comfortably about little things with parents is the child who may turn first to his folks when confronted with a large problem. (And if you are having trouble getting chats started, try doing something else at the same time—driving, drying dishes, raking a lawn with Teen avoids the "lecture format" and lets conversation sprout more casually.)

3. Be alert to "talk turn-offs." From time to time, listen to your own voice, and ask yourself if you'd speak to a friend the way you're conferring with Teen. If not, why not? Ask yourself: Do I talk longer than a minute without giving Junior Higher a chance to speak? (If his eyes tend to glaze over whenever your mouth opens, the answer is probably "yes.") Do I correct inconsequential teen comments, giving the impression that facts are more important than feelings or ideas? Do I *usually* become argumentative or authoritative, or use "conversation chillers" such as, "When I was your age . . ." or "You kids today think . . ."? Do I become easily distracted by the TV or telephone, giving Teen the idea that I was just killing time with him until something more interesting came along?

4. Don't take you child's occasional rejection personally. It hurts when someone we love turns away, apparently preferring others to our company, casting aside the gestures of goodwill and kindness that we offer. This is the time when some parents are tempted to vacillate, to abandon their principles in order to be more popular with their youngsters or express irrational anger at being rejected.

But it is natural for the junior high child to retreat. He is predictably inconsistent right now, and he often retreats in a hurtful way. But this phase will not last forever. As the teenager grows, he discovers more tactful, pleasant ways of asserting his maturity. It is a mistake for parent to relax their standards, just to win their teenagers back. Popularity with their children will *not* follow as a result, and the stability of the household will be threatened.

Instead, when your child is in a secretive or critical mood, try to remain outwardly calm and unaffected by it all. Avoid constant yelling. Your child already lives in a high-decibel world and really isn't impressed with noise, unless it's infrequent. Maintain your dignity, develop outside interests, and try to be a mature model. It won't be easy, of course, but what worthwhile activity ever is?

CHANGING RELATIONSHIPS WITH SIBLINGS

Parents aren't the only ones who find a junior high schooler trying; he leaves his mark on his siblings too, especially those in grade school. Although a teenager despises nagging when it's directed at *him*, he sees no harm in finding fault with everything the younger generation does. His little sister is a "spoiled brat" because she ate the last of the chocolate ice cream which he had, of course, reserved for himself. His younger brother is a "wimp" because he's getting an A in math while older brother is barely passing. Your teenager's main thrust here is to improve the behavior of these pathetic creatures. The fact that his own behavior could stand a little work never seems to occur to him.

Kids of this age do seem to get along better with older siblings, but those just a few years younger drive them crazy. Peace often requires effort and negotiations, so Mr. Junior High usually isn't motivated to seek it. It's more satisfying simply to slam a door. He loves toddlers and preschoolers, however, and it's not hard to see why. They're cute, non-threatening, rarely fight back, and besides, they think he's wonderful. This two-way devotion makes some junior high kids the most reliable and clever babysitters any family can find. (And often leads to a neighbor telling you how marvelous your Jimmy is while you, bewildered, wonder if you're both talking about the same child.)

THE PEER GROUP

Your teenage daughter's favorite age group, of course, is her classmates. As she struggles to break free from your control, she also realizes that the risk of standing alone is too great. Another support system must provide security. And she finds it among her peers.

Most studies show that in junior high school the peer group's influence is about equal with that of Mom and Dad. By the onset of high school, the peer group becomes predominant and will continue to be so throughout the next several years. The statistic means that, given the chance to follow the groups' ideas or her parents', the child will *prefer* to go with the gang.

She may not always *do* so, for reasons we will discuss later, but the desire is there, and the strength of the peer group cannot be underestimated.

Kids in their early teens crave a great deal of attention, but on the other hand they don't want to stand out from the crowd. Nothing is more devastating to Thirteen than to be singled out for punishment, or even praise, in the classroom, or to be considered different in any way. That willingness to be different and make up one's own mind will come later, when values have been clarified and confidence has increased. For now, however, security comes from being just like everyone else. If peer acceptance is almost synonymous with self-acceptance at this age, pity the poor boy who is a foot taller than everyone else, the girl who matures too early or—worse yet—too late, the child who enjoys poetry when everyone else hates it. These "loners" may feel ostracized and completely "out of it," even though their feelings have no basis in fact. Or the group may consciously exclude a certain classmate as evidence of group power, power that none would have as individuals. Much that happens in school—athletics, grades, elections—is based on competition, and by junior high, most kids' memories are filled with failures. More C's than A's, more games lost than won, other kids with bigger bedrooms, nicer clothes, more Little League trophies ... One would logically assume that children who have experienced the pain of rejection or failure would refuse to inflict the same sort of difficulty on another, but such is not the case in junior high.

"I just hate it when kids gang up on each other," says a junior high principal. "*They* want to be part of a gang—it's crucial to them—but then they turn around and ostracize someone else. It's another example of their inconsistent thinking." Because peer group acceptance is so vital at this age, any small development that appears to threaten it can throw a teenage girl into agony. A pimple on her chin, short hair when long is the rule, jeans from Sears instead of the designer popular at the moment, all are grounds for chronic humiliation, the feeling that she will never fit in. And without fitting in, where will her security come from, now that she's moved beyond the security of Mom and Dad?

THE FRIENDLESS CHILD

Parents often complain about peers and their influence, but the opposite side of the coin can be equally tough—a son or daughter who has no peers. Psychologists estimate that between 5 and 10% of elementary-school kids are literally friendless, some actively disliked and the butt of cruel jokes, a larger group dubbed "invisibles," kids who are not necessarily ostracized, but instead overlooked, rarely included in recess huddles or invited to parties.

The lonely preadolescent is in a tough spot. For although most classroom friendships won't last into adulthood, the feelings they generate will. A younger child may have been able to assuage isolation with family protection, hobbies and other trade-offs, but in junior high, as we've seen, the peer group assumes paramount importance. While kids' opinions of each other change rapidly, researchers believe that those who stay unpopular for long periods, becoming convinced that they are somehow unworthy of attention, may be at risk for relationship difficulties later in life.

Why are some kids singled out for rejection? Sometimes they're victims of their own behavior, needing help in handling conflict, merging their actions with the group or learning to be supportive of one another. One researcher founds that disenfranchised kids taunt and threaten classmates more often, push, argue or exhaust peers with constant negative feedback. Most aren't purposely obnoxious, just less sensitive to how peers might feel. Other disliked kids have good social skills generally, but can't handle a certain kind of situation—crying when teased, for example, or flaring into temper during an athletic competition.

Some parents believe that an ostracized child should "tough it out" on his own. But that's not always wise. A better course might be to ask a child's teacher for her observations; teachers cannot be social directors, but they can subtly turn class rejection into a degree of acceptance by setting certain behavior standards for the group-at-large, as well as giving an unpopular child an occasional job or (subdued) notice or thanks. Junior high teachers are adept at spotting reasons for unpopularity too, and can give parents a tactful bird's-eye view of what's really going on. Some sessions with the school psychologist may also help. Kids need to see that their parents are concerned enough about them to discuss difficulties with other experts. In some cases, however, things cannot be improved (at least not right away), and the best we can do for the socially-wounded youngster is to equip him to handle his pain, and give him reassurance of our own unconditional acceptance. This is difficult because often, parents report feeling angry at their child's social backwardness. Others endure Preteen's victimization as if the child within the adult self was being assaulted once again. "I was bullied as a youngster, just like my sixth-grade son," reports one dad. "And when it happened to him, I was flooded with all the feelings of rage and helplessness that I thought I'd successfully buried. All I wanted Jeremy to do was to knock that kid's block off."

Wisely, this father instead shared his own memories of feeling helpless and angry with his son, and Jeremy gained new perspective, and realized he wasn't alone, that Dad understood more than Jeremy thought.

Although solutions don't come easily right now, the more input kids have in solving social problems, the more valuable the lesson seems to be. Rather than seeking to impose solutions, an adult can ask, "What do you need to feel better? What do you think would happen if . . .?"

For example, one twelve-year-old begged to transfer schools to avoid a clique that was making her miserable. "What will happen if you have the same problem at the new school?" her mother asked. "Then I'll know it's me," the girl matter-of-factly replied. She was taking responsibility—and she was permitted to transfer. (It worked out well.)

About a third of all rejected kids stay unpopular during high school, but for the rest, these are better years. They're able to master enough social skills to find a place in the peer group hierarchy. Invisibles fare better; the vast majority find a niche in the high school band, newspaper or debating team. As in many instances, time does heal.

FADS

This need to fit in explains why young teenagers want to look and dress identically. There are so many episodes in Janey's life that she *can't* control right now, but she can at least make sure that her shoes, shirt, and raincoat pass the crowd test. Or can she?

We parents often tend to balk at these unreasonable fads, refusing to see why it matters if Janey wears discount sneakers or a pair from a high-priced boutique. But to her it does matter terribly. In Janey's mind those shoes may be the price of admission into the all-important peer group. They've become a symbol of her own self-acceptance. Never again will the correct label take on such significance.

Since clothes, hairstyles and other fads *are* so important, parents can use them as powerful bargaining tools, trade-offs for more important items. As several parents explain: "I told John that his hair length was completely up to him. But he had to keep it clean."

"When my girls balked at going to church, I delved deeper and discovered that it wasn't the service they disliked—it was the fact that I insisted they dress up and sit with the family. We compromised—they wear jeans now, and sit a few pews behind us. I don't think the Lord minds, and we're happy too."

"We explained to Kathy that our budget just couldn't handle more than $25 for a pair of jeans, but if she wanted the designer label, she was perfectly free to earn the difference in cost by babysitting. She did."

In all of these examples, parents treated the child's need seriously rather than ridiculing it. They defused a potentially explosive situation yet kept their own standards intact. And along the way they gently reminded the teenager that material possessions aren't nearly as important as the kind of person one is. Kids won't agree with this now, but they do need to hear it. As the peer group solidifies, its quest becomes "to be noticed." And as with a two-year-old throwing a tantrum, negative attention is better than no attention at all. The kids travel in a loud, boisterous pack, behaving in ways they wouldn't dream of if alone. (Don't sit next to them in movie theaters or restaurants.) Boys practice swaggering, to accompany their newfound tough-guy image. Girls wear lots of eye makeup and conduct conversations in high-decibel range, punctuated by ear-splitting screams. If an adult calls attention to their obnoxious behavior, so much the better. Obviously, the secret is to ignore most of it (as one does with a two-year-old tantrum-thrower) and to comment primarily on positive, mature behavior—if and when you can find it.

SLANG AND SWEARING

Junior high ushers in the use of slang in full force. Kids seem to develop their own language, and parents are hard-pressed to decipher the code. Even the most common sentences become mysterious; strange phrases dot the conversational landscape. It's annoying, but if possible, remember your own teen slang and try to ignore theirs.

It's not so easy to ignore swearing, however. Bad language is another trademark of the junior high set which, unfortunately, does persist through high school. A teenager's vocabulary can make a felon blush. It's mainly designed, of course, to provoke and shock adults and to show the world how "cool" the kids are. Although the use of profanity is one of the many things you can't control when your child is away from home, you *can* take a stand within your own household. No family has an obligation to tolerate teenage vulgarities or mouthiness, even though "everyone else talks that way."

Tell your youngster that he is polluting your environment, setting a terrible example for his younger siblings, and displaying his own ignorance and immaturity when he swears. Obscenities lose a lot of their shock value when no one is around to hear them, so tell him that if he insists on speaking this way, he will have to do it in his bedroom, behind closed doors. He will be perfectly welcome to join the family circle whenever he decides to clean up his act. Then be sure to follow through. Watch your own language, too; there's no use chastising a teen for using gutter words if they're a part of your own repertoire.

SHOPLIFTING

Although stealing is an activity that can occur at any age, it often becomes frequent in junior high when, as we've seen, peer group pressure is at its most intense, and interest in clothes, magazines and other adolescent paraphernalia peaks. Kids hang out at malls, then gradually "lift" a lipstick, a shirt, even stereo components, increasing the lure as success continues. Then one day the bubble bursts. A store detective spots your child stuffing something into her purse, takes her to the security office and calls the police who sometimes handcuff her and lead her through the store as curious shoppers gawk. She is taken to the police station, searched, fingerprinted, photographed and perhaps put in a jail cell until her distraught parents arrive. Why do kids do it? The answers are as varied as the shoplifters themselves. "It's almost like a game of chance," one fourteen-year-old admitted, "and I kept winning." Others impulsively submit to dares from the group, enjoy getting something for nothing, or steal out of a need to have an item that might buy popularity or respect. Although most would view stealing from a parent or friend as wrong, they rationalize shoplifting by telling themselves that since a store has so much merchandise, no one will really be hurt.

Police departments and stores have various policies on shoplifting. In some cases, especially if it's a first offense, Teen may be required to meet with representatives of the store to confess and apologize, or may be sent for counseling, fined or released on probation. The law is unevenly applied, and in some areas of the country, young shoplifters could actually be placed in foster care or detention homes. Whatever the disposition, your child might have a police record which will affect her ability to be hired, perhaps, or breach trust built up with family or friends over the years.

The subject of shoplifting ought to be discussed around your family dinner table in objective terms, long before the possibility actually exists. Your preteen should know what the penalties are, as well as being exposed to the idea of the humiliation, ridicule and fear she would also suffer as a result of being arrested. It's also important to stress that, occasionally, innocent people are also accused of taking merchandise (especially if they're part of a noisy irritating group) and need to know what to do in such a situation. Tell your child to stay calm, don't threaten or try to get away, don't be bullied into confessing something she didn't do and make sure you are contacted as quickly as possible.

Getting caught stealing can be humiliating and frightening, but *not* getting caught is even worse. Exposure can keep a child from heading down a path of dishonesty, put an end to her association with unhealthy companions, force parent and child to talk about issues that may, up to now, have been ignored, help Preteen decide what kind of person she wants to be, how she will handle temptation the next time and perhaps even help her learn more direct ways of asking for the help she needs and is entitled to have.

SAME-SEX FRIENDSHIPS

In junior high boys usually flock together to talk about sports and tell dirty jokes, while girls team up in intimate groups to compare notes, chat incessantly, scream and giggle. There is not much one-to-one mingling of the sexes now, and parents shouldn't encourage it in the form of early dating, paired boy-girl parties, or occasions that throw youngsters into artificial adult social settings. Junior high kids are more comfortable in groups, using each other for support. They still need time to grow into more mature relationships.

Same-sex friendships flourish now, especially with one or two special pals. They are a necessary step toward the development of normal boy-girl relationships later, a step that *cannot* be skipped. If it fails to occur in junior high, it will take place later. In this stage teenagers can be quite intense in their friendships, quite physically affectionate too; psychologists often refer to a latent homosexual stage. This *doesn't* mean that your daughter is becoming a lesbian just because she has a deep, close friendship with another girl or feels strong hero-worship for a female teacher, a movie starlet, or other female role model, which also happens frequently. Instead it seems to be nature's way of letting these deep, loving feelings develop in a safe, socially acceptable way. At a later date, when a teen is more mature, she can subconsciously allow herself to direct these now familiar feelings toward a boy, thus initiating the male-female relationship. Because your child is probably aware of homosexuality, she may be secretly afraid that her attraction to her girlfriends means something is wrong with her. You can reassure her by mentioning that there is a vast difference between "feeling" and "doing," and that soon she will progress to the boy/girl experience.

Since both sexes like to be around each other, this age is perfect for socializing while involved in constructive projects. Schools that offer newspapers, choral groups, banks, and even mixed-team sports give kids a chance to mingle in comfortable ways.

JOBS

Junior high kids also like the idea of earning some of their own spending money. While higher-paying part-time jobs are not yet available to them, they can deliver newspapers, babysit, caddy, cut lawns, shovel snow, walk dogs, and develop other neighborhood services.

At first, such windfalls will simply supplement Thirteen's regular allowance, and perhaps allow the purchase of a coveted camera or pair of designer jeans. As your daughter begins earning more regularly, however, she should be expected to spend a portion of her income on daily expenses, and even buy an article of necessary clothing from time to time.

Parents who do not need financial assistance from their offspring often object at this point, believing that Daughter should have the right to spend her earnings any way she wants (especially when they are so meager). But such an attitude is mistaken because, as many experts agree, work values seem to get lost when kids toil strictly for their own material extras, rather than contributing in some way to the family, as youngsters did years ago. One way to preserve that ethic—to make a job less the pursuit of "stuff" and more the means of self-discipline and pride—is to allow a youngster the satisfaction of chipping in to the household pot. She does this, for more affluent parents, not by paying an electric bill or buying extra groceries but by covering some of her own expenses now, and as her income increases, saving for college or other large-ticket items.

Mom and Dad can encourage this activity by gradually cutting back on the allowance. Thirteen may protest a bit, but her emerging feelings of pride and self-sufficiency will eventually carry her through the rough spots. Despite our bank balances, we should also make sure she knows how much we appreciate her contribution, and how impressed we are with her growing maturity. Parents should also take care not to criticize Thirteen's spending habits harshly during this first taste of independence. A youngster who is contributing to her own financial well-being has the right to make some spending decisions, even if a few do turn out to be disasters. That's how she'll learn to handle money more wisely.

Junior high schoolers can be maddeningly inconsistent. But they are at the gateway to growth. There your daughter sits, watching TV cartoons, hugging her stuffed panda, grinning at something her baby brother just said. Tonight at grade-school graduation she'll be wearing a grown-up dress and pantyhose, her manner aloof and serious. Neither little girl nor woman, she's working hard to shed her childish cocoon, to become her own person at last. Now we give her roots, security, consistency in her everchanging life. And someday, someday soon, we will give her wings.

Chapter 2

Freshman:
The Year of Experimentation

> *They have exalted notions because they have not yet been humbled by life or learned necessary limitations . . . They think themselves equal to great things. They would rather do noble deeds than useful ones, their lives are regulated more by moral feeling than by reasoning—all their mistakes are in the direction of doing things excessively and vehemently. They overdo everything—they love too much and hate too much."*
> Aristotle, c. 320 B.C.

The first day of high school, a moment fraught with anxiety, uncertainty, and plenty of enthusiasm, too. (In some parts of the country the middle, or junior high, school covers grades 7-9; high school, grades 10-12. A teenager in such a school may live through "Freshman" experiences in his "Sophomore" year—his *first* year of high school.) It's natural for your teenager to have mixed emotions about this venture. He feels apprehension, of course. Till now, he has viewed the high school scene from a distance. Its campus seemed massive, its students sophisticated, its courses intimidating, the whole atmosphere surrounded by a mystique he wasn't old enough to penetrate.

And today he's a part of it. Will he fit in? Can he cope with this challenging lifestyle? Can he balance grades, friends, extracurricular activities? And how will he find his way around the building? From the position of eighth-grade kingpin, your child is catapulted into his role as underling, the lowest of the low—a freshman.

But he feels excitement too. For high school, beyond any doubt, signifies the end of childhood. It is society's official admission that this youngster has passed a particular test of behavior and left certain boundaries behind, that he will henceforth be treated in a different manner, in keeping with his new stature. Despite a few reservations, a youngster happily casts aside the restrictions of yesterday and looks forward to preparing for adulthood.

A high school freshman abandons negative behavior, too. At least for a while, his attitude has changed. Muted is the supercritical, sometimes hostile stance of the junior high years. Fourteen does have his problems, but he appears to handle them more cheerfully much of the time. Like the sunny three-year-old after the stormy "terrible two's," many freshmen enjoy a period of relative peace, a zest and excitement for living that overshadows their darker moods.

THE CHALLENGE OF HIGH SCHOOL

First of all, there is so much to occupy them. By the time they graduated, they had learned all they ever needed or wanted to know about grade school. But high school presents an entirely new learning environment and experience, and they must begin at the bottom again. Freshmen are not always ready to meet the stresses of high school, especially if it is a large, complicated facility. Usually their biggest problems are managing their time properly and keeping track of their possessions. Mastering these challenges, even if no others came along, could become a full-time job that keeps freshman energy levels at fever pitch.

High school means remembering to bring a gym suit (or bathing suit) every day, not just once or twice a week. It means learning combinations for a variety of lockers, and storing textbooks, assignments, supplies, and lunch in them instead of a desk. That means planning ahead: "Do I take my Science book now for third hour, or do I run back for it between first and second?" It means finding one's way through a maze of corridors only to be late for class, and having to go to the principal's office for an admission slip (if upperclassmen don't direct one onto the football field instead). And worst of all, it means being short. Once the logistics have been handled, the freshman has to cope with more. High school means having six different teachers for six courses and adjusting individually to each class routine and each personality. (And finding that Biology is absolutely impossible, and Algebra is even worse.) High school means long-range assignments—a term paper due in October, a Math assignment finished by Friday—rather than homework completed each night for the following day. (And how does one *remember* the term paper due date?) High school means taking responsibility for one's own work. A grammar school teacher might have hounded Thirteen for that overdue book report, but Fourteen is on his own. No book report—no grade.

High school is a also smorgasbord of extracurricular ventures, each headed by a teacher who believes his team or activity is the most important one in the school, and each expecting a body-and-soul commitment from Teen. Are you going to join the band, Freshman? You'll need to keep track of your instrument, your sheet music, a 21-piece uniform. You'll have to show up for rehearsals for football and basketball half-time, perform in several marching competitions and concerts, and—oh yes—wash cars to raise funds. Thinking of joining the tennis team? We expect promptness at all practices, a clean uniform, an aggressive, competitive spirit, and—oh yes—consider taking private lessons at a nearby tennis club, too. How about the debate club? We practice two afternoons a week. Library research is on your own time, of course, the bus leaves for tournaments at 7 p.m. sharp, and—oh yes—we expect to win a trophy tonight!

At this point, the beginning freshman has no idea which of these goodies will appeal to him. He'd like to taste all of them, if possible. But how will he find any time left over to eat, sleep, breathe, and visit the orthodontist?

PEER GROUP RESTRUCTURING

High school also means an intricate restructuring of the peer group, for not everyone from the old gang will be attending the new school. And among those who do, the remaining peer group will splinter and reform around particular interests rather than the neighborhood.

"We have several 'types' at school, each with subgroups according to grade level," explains a student. "There are the jocks, the real athletic guys who date the cheerleaders. They usually have good grade point averages, win a lot of awards, and are school heroes. Then there are the burnouts—they hang around outside school, keep their jackets open even during freezing weather, smoke, cut classes, and act scruffy."

"Actually," another teenager adds, "the jocks probably drink and party more than the burnouts—who are more into pot—but drinking is acceptable when the jocks do it."

"Then," First Student continues, "there are gangs that stick together because of shared interests. The band kids are a group, and the auto freaks and the thespians—the ones who get all the leads in the plays . . ."

"They're usually into punk and act sophisticated . . . "

"Every group dresses just a little different, like preppies or old jeans or the punk look. And finally there are the loners, the kids who are often the brains of the school. They keep to themselves and sometimes act as if they don't want to be around anyone ..."

"But I'm not sure that's true . . ."

THE WRONG CROWD

Jockeying for position and acceptance in a new peer group, which is assuming more importance than ever before, can be exhausting and fraught with risk for the freshman. For what will she do if she is rejected? Remember, the gang provides security and feelings of well-being in large measure. How will she cope if there is no place for her?

"This is one explanation of how a kid can get in with the wrong crowd," explains a high school science teacher. "She reaches out to one or two groups and feels rejected. Perhaps they ignore her at lunch, or laugh at her in class. Then she may try again, this time with a gang whose price of admission is smoking pot or cutting class. The kid wants to be accepted so badly that she's willing to conform, even if this behavior goes against her code."

While no psychologist underestimates the power of the peer group, many feel that the *less* approval a teen gets at home, the *more* she will seek it from the group. So the watchword for parents is obvious: Approve of your child and make sure she knows it. "It's perfectly permissible for parents to reject a teen's *behavior*," the science teacher points out, "but they should never reject the teen herself. There's a vast difference between 'Can you study harder and bring this D up to a C?' and 'You're a failure—you just don't care, do you?' One approach indicates disapproval of performance, but the other, quite devastating, is rejection of the person. And if the teen gets a constant message that she isn't any good, then why not hang out with the losers—she fits, doesn't she?"

It's hard for parents to decide what to do when they don't like one or more of their teen's pals. Do we step in and stop the relationship (and can we actually do so?) or stand back and let Son or Daughter make their own decisions?

Although each conclusion must be based on individual circumstances, parents might benefit from some rules of thumb other Moms and Dads have used:

• If you have no concrete reasons for disapproval, let your teen choose his own friends. Even though you think that Sam-down-the-street might be a far more suitable pal than that scruffy drummer your boy inexplicably likes, hold your tongue. There may be lots of negative things about Sam that your son has decided not to share with you; or he may simply be drawn to a friend whose outward appearance belies a heart of gold. Remember too that adolescence is a time to experiment with many different kinds of companions and activities, and a friendship that *doesn't* work out can teach as many valuable lessons as one that does. Be aware that your vaguely negative feelings may be based on stereotypes, prejudice or even a dislike of a certain fad; such reasons are really not enough to banish Scruffy Drummer from Son's life.

• If you spot signs of *potential* trouble, increase your vigilance. For example, many teens today come from homes where both parents work full-time (or are being raised by a working mom); thus, housekeys are often passed around so kids can gain access to an empty environment in which to drink, play hookey or have sex. If your teen socializes mostly with peers who have little or no supervision, you'll need to keep a closer watch. Or what if a pal has gotten into trouble (shoplifting, skipping school) but has apparently mended his ways? You don't want to ostracize a child who's made a mistake, but you need to be sure that your own offspring isn't being pulled into undesirable activities. It helps to share your concerns with your teen: "I'm not completely pleased about your association with Judy, but I'm willing to keep an open mind on it, as long as you all stay out of trouble."

• If your freshman is definitely gravitating toward the wrong crowd—a group of kids whose values and activities you believe are wrong for her—*now* is the time to take a firm hand. The longer you delay, the more entrenched her position will become. If discussions between you yield no reason why your child prefers this group, or you can't come to an agreeable solution, turn first to your teen's high school guidance counselor. He's on the scene and can more accurately evaluate the potential for harm. If this doesn't help, consider family counselling. To break your teen's dependence on this group, you must discover why she feels drawn to them and work from there. Punishment may work for a time, but if the underlying causes aren't discovered and addressed, the problem will continue, and may very well get worse.

TRYING ON NEW BEHAVIOR

Because your freshman's world is so new, and because he wants to taste and see and learn everything about it, freshman year is often called the year of *experimentation*. As a junior high student, he was primarily inconsistent, and while he still has periods of highs and lows, they are not quite so intense or dramatic now. The roller coaster syndrome quietly gives way to the need to discover who he is and what he wants to be, through school, through friends, through various activities. He continues to pull away from his parents, but while he did so *verbally* in the junior high years, now he will put some action behind his words. He will "try on" several different ways of behaving to discover which ones are right for him. Although he will do it cheerfully much of the time, your freshman will undoubtedly *experiment*.

Experimentation takes many forms. Some of it is quite harmless, although it can be mystifying or annoying to the older generation. Some can lead to disaster if not checked by authority figures. It is best if Fourteen is allowed to experiment from a base of emotional security which has been provided by parents throughout his life. Emotional security implies certain limits ("Because we love you, we can't allow you to do this"), but it also grants some freedom ("You are growing up and you have the right to make some decisions on your own"). If either of these two components is missing, the teen will flounder, and either experiment too wildly or decide that the risk of experimentation is too great, thus limiting his growth.

The best atmosphere of emotional security is *strict* on behavior but very *permissive* about feelings. "It's okay to be mixed up sometimes, to wonder and worry and be angry or sad. But it's not okay to cheat, abuse or hurt others, because of your feelings." A fourteen-year-old is experiencing many feelings that are new to him. Sometimes he can't even put these feelings into words. But when he can express them, he should be allowed to do so, without threat of punishment, arguments, or constant disagreement. If upset always follows, a teen will soon stop trying to talk. And that's a shame, because parents can be a terrific sounding board for teens, against which kids can test ideas, theories, and observations without actually having to experience everything.

So, if possible, strive to make your home environment an accepting, loving place where your children are allowed to discuss any subject they please. Don't automatically assume they are gravitating toward bad behavior just because they talk about it. You think out loud sometimes, too, don't you? Don't preach, act like a "heavy," or try to force your own principles down their throats. You'll only silence kids at a time when communication could be valuable. You will, of course, express your own opinions calmly, and sometimes you will have to match your views with action. But remember, experimenting means trying on new ideas and values, defining oneself. In the long run, your teen may embrace your own way of life, but his beliefs will feel more *his* if he has been able to reach them by himself.

TAKING RISKS

Teens experiment by taking risks. Some of these risks, as we've mentioned, seem ludicrous or annoying to the adult world. Others can be a source of real problems. What are some of the risks freshmen are willing to take, in order to find out more about themselves?

"Almost everything is a risk to freshmen," explains a guidance counselor. "Since they're still on a roller coaster to some extent, and since they want so badly to belong, the least little fancied slight is agony. I tell them they can't be like turtles, hiding inside a safe familiar shell. They have to learn to stick their necks out now and then."

What are typical risks for a freshman?

• Daring to wear a skirt when everyone else prefers jeans.

• Raising one's hand in class to answer a question. ("What if the teach rejects my statement, which feels like she's rejecting *me*, or what if the kids laugh?")

• Saying "hi" to a popular kid in the hallway. ("Will she answer or just walk past?")

• Joining a club, especially one that is considered "out."

• Being seen with a particular person, or telling others that one likes this person.

The list goes on and on.

"Freshmen are very *real* people," one teacher comments. "They haven't yet learned the art of covering up, of disguising their attitudes. That's why their feelings seem so up-and-down. This cover-up happens as they go along and mature. They learn that revealing too much of themselves may hurt, and they're becoming more sensitive to rejection."

Freshmen girls, say teachers, are into nitty-gritty issues. They're not afraid to share ideas. They like to analyze their problems, telling twenty-five different versions of the same event. And if an older boy walks into the room, they'll giggle, poke each other, and whisper. If they're noticed, it makes their whole day. Contrast this attitude with the days of junior high, when being noticed was anathema, except as part of a group. Freshmen boys, on the other hand, are "squirrely and hard to pin down," says a youth counselor. They seem scared of their emotions, he observes, and tend to stay away from personal encounters. When talking of problems, a boy will encapsulate everything.

"Most freshmen boys are so *small*," adds a teacher, "and they seem intensely concerned about everything. They come to the desk hesitantly—'Um, uh . . . should this be a comma or a semi-colon?' They need approval with everything."

If a well-endowed girl comes to school in a revealing halter and walks confidently across the room, all eyes will follow her, girls' as well as boys'. "It's curiosity and envy," the same teacher said. "They all realize that she's strutting her stuff—and she has stuff!"

Although freshman boys and girls manifest their concerns through different styles of behavior, their concerns remain the same: Who am I? What do I like? Where do I fit in? The answers to these questions may take years to discover, but the search for personal identity is well under way. Through experimenting with different ways of behaving, observing others and daring to stick one's neck out again and again, the personality deepens, the growth process moves along. If only parents remembered how difficult it is to be a freshman!

MAKING STATEMENTS AT HOME

The risk of experimentation goes on at home too, but here the questions that teenagers probe are a bit different: What are my limits? What can I get away with? What behavior is important enough to my parents to get a reaction from them, good or bad? Here in the relative safety of their homes, freshmen try on new modes of living. Each is designed to make a statement about themselves, to indicate that they are people too, with their own ideas. One of the most popular (and irritating) statements teens choose to make is in the area of their home turf: their bedrooms. Sometime around the high school period, most teen bedrooms become a stomach-turning exhibit of crumpled papers, decaying apples, strewn cosmetics, milk-encrusted glasses, and unmade beds. The boy who lifts weight to build his biceps cannot summon up enough strength to toss his rancid socks into the laundry hamper. The girl who must clear a path of dirty (and clean) clothes to get from her door to her window complains that she has "nothing to wear." A child who takes three showers a day may wear the same pair of unwashed denims for a week.

The media's influence is strong and freshmen still worship heroes, so bedroom walls (like school lockers) are plastered with posters. Bare-chested macho guys in jeans ads, sultry starlets from popular TV shows, sports figures and rock stars stare out from every available inch of wall space.

With bizarre music, of course, high school students make another statement. If a stereo or disc player is buried somewhere in the litter of a teen's room, chances are it's beating out the kind of music that makes a parent's teeth hurt. If the boy or girl has a personal TV, it will be on at the same time as the stereo (and your juvenile will earnestly assure you that he *can* do his homework in the midst of the din). In many homes, a separate phone line is also standard procedure for the kids, leading to eager and tireless communication, especially among girls. At every available interlude, the telephone transmits the endless trivia which is somehow meaningful to this age group. Although basic family relationships are more cordial during freshman year, a teenager's bedroom (or "stable," as one father put it) can become the source of many family outbursts.

How do seasoned parents handle it?

"Kids try like crazy to shock us, to let us know that they don't accept all our standards," one mother explains, "and I've learned to let them have the satisfaction of doing just that—in areas that really don't matter in the long run. Sometimes there's value in making an issue over little things, just to defuse the kids' need to shock. Then life never gets to the big issues." This mother carries on a bit now and then about the upstairs pigpens. "It secretly pleases them to know their 'statement' is annoying me," she says. But most of the time she keeps their doors closed and ignores the mess. "I know they'll outgrow the slob scene as soon as they finance their own furniture."

"We all excavate together when the piles get too high," says another, "but I feel it usually isn't worth arguing about. If I let the kids get away with it in minor matters, they usually accept my authority when the issue is grave."

One mother points out that since freshmen are so disorganized and distractible, she's putting her efforts into streamlining her daughter's environment rather than her room. "A teen phone may save the rest of the family a lot of aggravation," says she, "but I'm convinced a freshman isn't mature enough for the privilege. It's too much of a distraction and so is a personal TV, and our daughter has neither." This girl isn't nagged about the condition of her room, but she is expected to spend school nights from 8 to 10 p.m. *in* it. No phone calls are made or accepted, no TV shows watched, although rock music, at low volume, is permitted. "I'm structuring her time for her right now," Mom explains, "giving her the opportunity for two quiet hours of study each night. Since she isn't capable of saying no to her friends at this stage, I do it for her. She tells me how old-fashioned I am, but secretly, she's relieved to have some of the pressure taken off." What teen hasn't frantically signaled his parent to say "no" while he pretends to say "yes" on the phone? It's great when Mom or Dad takes the rap, leaving Teen's crowd-security intact!

Other suggestions for coping with the teenage bedroom blues?

1. Try to avoid cleaning it, unless Aunt Tillie's coming for a visit or you have to sort the change-of-season clothes or you're looking for Son under the rumpled bedding. It's going to frustrate Son, coming home each day to an immaculate room and a foiled statement, and he's going to *have* to look for another way to emphasize his independence. And perhaps this new way may be a lot more harmful.

2. In keeping with family standards of modesty or morality, there may be certain posters or record albums to which you can rightfully object. But if the stuff seems only mildly obnoxious, let Son enjoy it. He has a right to spend his allowance or earnings on his own choices. It's all part of the image.

3. Since your child wants to be independent, and also seems to want to abuse his clothing, help him along by *refusing* to do his laundry. He's old enough to learn the difference between bleach and bluing. After you've conducted a crash course on the washer and dryer, step aside. When your child awakens to a morning when he indeed has "nothing to wear," he'll learn to take better care of his clothes.

Actually, by this age, your child should be capable of handling many household chores—cooking simple meals, grocery shopping, mending, and cleaning. These are also experiments in practical living, and it's well worth an occasional burnt dinner or foolish purchase in order to learn. One study showed that only one-third of freshman college students who dropped out did so because of failing grades; the rest were unable to handle things like self-discipline, study habits, checking accounts, and laundry. Young people should be given these responsibilities gradually, at home, so they won't be overwhelmed by eventual freedom.

DRINKING

Messy rooms, loud music, endless telephone calls are annoying but harmless experiments in living and growing. But some experiments can lead to tragedy—and the most popular one at this age is drinking.

To teenagers, alcohol is a symbol of maturity. It simulates sophistication, "coolness," and defiance of authority. Some experts believe that the more rebellious a teen is, the earlier he will try alcohol. But *all* agree that drinking now starts at an earlier age than ever before. "If the age of alcohol experimentation gets any younger," says one counselor wryly, "it'll be prenatal."

In order to prevent juvenile drinking, many schools sponsor programs on drug and alcohol abuse, some starting as early as fourth grade. Parents need to become informed as well, and they need to examine their own attitudes and drinking habits, preferably prior to the time when they will be required to handle the subject with their teenagers.

Many experts also feel that occasionally serving alcohol in the home to youngsters in controlled settings, such as wine at a family banquet, takes much of the mystique out of it. By divesting alcohol of its forbidden status, treating it naturally and instructing a youngster in proper use, the air of mystery is dissipated. "How can a kid use alcohol to rebel, if he's allowed to have an occasional beer at home?" asks a teacher. "It's lost the force of an issue, especially if parents treat it as something that is fine, as long as it's not abused."

Authorities believe that several factors today cause young kids to turn to alcohol and abuse it. Peer pressure may enter into the picture, if alcohol gives them access to a group. Easy availability makes a big difference: almost any can obtain alcoholic beverages these days, at prices cheaper than other drugs. Role models may actually encourage teenage drinking. The cocktail hour is an American institution, and many teen heroes portray drinking as "cool." Finally, feelings of alienation may lead a teen to drink. Youngsters who feel lost, frustrated, or alienated from society or their families seek a temporary release from those pains through "getting high." "I believe that extreme alcohol use is always indicative of a problem in the home," says a high school guidance counselor. "This problem doesn't have to be major, such as the parents splitting up, or extreme poverty or abuse. Maybe Grandma lives with the family, and there isn't any privacy. Maybe there are lots of younger children, and the teen is made to feel like an unpaid servant. Maybe the parents are uptight, raised with the attitude that it's not right to talk about problems; they brush Teen off whenever he wants to air his gripes and communication fails."

"Teens may also feel that drunkenness allows them an excuse for bad behavior," theorizes another teacher. "They talk about 'how drunk I got' as if it were a badge of honor, a way of avoiding responsibility for sexual activity, silliness, fights or other activities which can result."

And perhaps the kids are reacting to parental indifference about alcohol. One survey shows that only 57% of the nation's adolescents have received any kind of parental instruction about the dangers of alcohol abuse. Worse, many parents are actually relieved if their children drink instead of taking drugs. And yet alcohol is a drug, too, which can have a devastating effect if not handled properly.

Large amounts of alcohol, like a six-pack of beer, which is equivalent to almost one-third of a fifth of whiskey or gin, can be detrimental to the development of the body, especially in growing youngsters. Studies indicate that young people become physically addicted more quickly than their elders. Driving while under the influence is a leading cause of traffic accidents, many of them fatal. And alcohol takes its toll in lost learning opportunities, undeveloped talents, the forfeit of a wholesome social life.

Not every teen who drinks alcohol is destined to abuse it. Some may not even try until late in high school, especially if the issue has been defused at home. But over 1.3 million American teens have a serious drinking problem, according to the National Institute on Alcohol Abuse and Alcoholism.

Many kids' initial experiments with alcohol occur during the summer between eighth-grade graduation and high school entry or sometime during freshman year. That same natural curiosity which is propelling your freshman toward many wholesome and worthwhile experiments may also urge him into seeing what happens when he drinks.

The first time your youngster tries alcohol can be a shock—for you, and for him, too. More than likely, he'll begin experimenting with beer. Because of the possible need for stealth and his own ignorance, he's apt to drink too quickly and too much. He will probably turn sick at his stomach, either at the drinking site or later on at home. Sometimes a burst of violent vomiting can put an end to further drinking "tests," at least for a time. Glassy-eyed, mumbling, wobbly on his feet, with breath smelling of mint, your son faces you and blatantly denies that he has been drinking. Shocked, you stare back, your thoughts in a turmoil. Not only is your child drunk, but he is also compounding the problem by lying. What can you do? And where have you failed?

Most likely you haven't failed at all, but how you handle this initial episode may have a bearing on your child's future drinking habits. Are you going to laugh it off, chalk it up to youthful adventurousness, consider it a harmless pastime, just part of growing up? Or will your teen be severely punished, forced to give up the friends who were also involved, made to work off several serious penalties before being allowed to leave the house again?

Neither approach will work that well. Alcohol *is* a serious matter, and to regard the first, or any, episode of drunkenness lightly gives your child the "green light" for more of the same. Where will it end? At what point *will* you be able to intervene successfully?

On the other hand, penalizing a teenager so severely for drinking that he will suffer the complete loss of freedom and friends is risky. He may react violently and seek out alcohol again, even if he isn't that interested, just to rebel against what he considers unfair treatment.

Instead, try to remember that the first brush with alcohol has been an experiment. Your teen was motivated mainly by curiosity. He has a distance to go before he becomes an abuser, and to treat him as an abuser *now* may create a problem larger than the one you already have.

Wait until the next day, when your son is capable of coherent conversation. Then get the particulars of the event from him. Where was the beer obtained? What friends were involved? How much did he consume? Your teen may be penitent, but he most likely will attempt to lie. You must keep at him, calmly but firmly, until you have the answers you need. You insistence on the truth shows him that you are taking the matter seriously, and also helps you to decide what action must be taken.

Once the entire story comes out, consider the facts. Was the liquor stolen, from a store, church, or home? If so, then restitution must be made. Your teen must learn that the rules of life don't change just because he is getting older. Was the drinking done in an empty home, or worse, with the consent of the parents throwing the party? This one is prickly. You may not wish to confront the parents with your views on the subject, but you probably will want to prohibit your son from visiting that home again, at least under the same circumstances. He may be secretly relieved.

Explain to your son that your concern is justified not only because alcohol can be dangerous, but also because he has betrayed your trust. He has acted in an irresponsible manner and he has also broken the law. Parents who provide liquor to minors are also breaking the law. The fact that he lied has further eroded your confidence in him. You understand that he was curious, perhaps influenced by his pals. You do wish to give the benefit of the doubt, and you're willing to give him a chance to redeem himself. But this situation cannot continue. What punishment does *he* feel is appropriate? What assurances can *he* offer about his future behavior?

Note that you are placing the responsibility where it belongs: on the teen's own shoulders. For it is his responsibility and his ultimate decision, a decision he will be faced with again and again during his high school years. You cannot chain him to his bed, prohibit him from leaving the house, cut him off from an outside life in order to keep him away from alcohol. Nor should you consider it your burden to intervene between his behavior and its consequences; to repeatedly "clean up" after your teen obscures valuable learning that might have taken place. Better that your child decide for himself what course of action to follow, and what he will do when faced with the next temptation.

Parental concern, coupled with an immediate but fair response, is often enough, at least for a while. Interestingly, many kids end up joining a school-sponsored chapter of SADD (Students Against Driving Drunk) or a similar club, designed to give them a supportive peer group and a way to handle temptation. Chances are, if your teen's self-image is strong, he will not feel the need to escape inner suffering by "getting high." Continue to be vigilant, however. The drinking problem surfaces again and again in high school, and it will have to be confronted again in a few years when your high school junior or senior gets his driver's license and goes to more parties.

If your counseling has little effect and your teenager continues to drink regularly, you probably are not going to be able to handle the problem on your own. Call on a professional support group. Contact your local chapter of Alcoholics Anonymous for advice; many chapters have special youth groups where teenage drinkers can meet with others of their own age. You can also investigate Al-Anon, an organization for those who live with problem drinkers. And Families Anonymous is especially designed for parents of teens in trouble, whether it be alcoholism, drug abuse, truancy, or other anti-social behavior. By listening to the techniques others are utilizing to help both their teens and themselves, you will find many answers.

MAGAZINES, R-RATED MOVIES

Freshmen are increasingly curious about sexual matters. But unless they are unusually precocious, they are not yet interested in experimenting personally. "Most freshmen regard sex as a never-never thing," one teacher observes. "They wouldn't be caught dead 'doing it.' By the time they're juniors, however, they're seeing intercourse as a possibility for themselves." Fourteen eagerly seeks out additional sex education. If Fourteens can get it through open discussions with parents, they're fortunate. Fourteen not only wants information, she also wants to discuss and evaluate it. She wants to know *why*, and she will also pick up many of her attitudes about sexuality by what she observes in her parents' relationship. Institutions can *reinforce* moral values, but they cannot give our children what we have not given them.

Unfortunately, the home is not the only place where teenagers absorb sexual values. The culture bombards our kids on all sides with attitudes that may conflict with our own. Teenagers can pick up all sorts of ideas from TV (especially the rise in availability of rented movie cassettes and R-rated cable stations), movies, magazines: sex is for fun, sex can make you popular, sex can be used to prove something. And if a teen is not adequately prepared, if controls have not been reinforced, she or he is often left to make choices independently.

Because freshmen are so curious about sexual matters, this is often the age when "girlie" magazines will accidentally be discovered under a boy's mattress. It's also the time when Fourteen pressures you for permission to attend R-rated movies. Both of these activities are typical of Fourteen's need to "find out" at a safe, secure distance.

There is nothing innately harmful in a freshman's desire to view naked bodies of the opposite sex. The problem is that certain magazines and movies can also portray attitudes, especially concerning women, that *are* harmful. Depicting females as objects of lust, as "things" to be used or hurt for physical pleasure, gives both boys and girls a distorted, one-dimensional view of sex, neglecting its profound richness. Movie violence, especially when it includes sexually sadistic episodes, emphasizes the sordid and bizarre aspects of life, rather than its wholesome pleasures.

In addition, such graphic visuals can sexually stimulate teenagers to the point that they have trouble holding their own desires in check. TV commercials and magazine ads are designed to be powerful stimulants of behavior; likewise the *content* of the TV shows, magazines, and movies that the ads accompany will influence behavior too. A recent study on cable TV viewing by a Michigan State researcher bolsters this claim; he found that exposure by college students to sexually-explicit contents resulted

in greater acceptance of promiscuity and sexual infidelity a-
mong both sexes. Fourteen- to sixteen-year-olds who were frequent television viewers judged sexually-oriented material more
acceptable and enjoyable than kids who logged fewer viewing
hours. Another study showed a relationship between the viewing of sex-oriented fare and the onset of sexual activity among
boys. Obviously, we adults must decide whether we wish to ex-
pose our teenagers to attitudes and stimulations that are drasti-
cally different from those we have provided in our homes.

In order to help adults make intelligent decisions when guiding our youth, The Motion Picture Association of America offers
four categories of film ratings. These ratings are published
alongside the newspaper movie ads, and posted in the theaters.

G—Generally acceptable for all ages. Includes Disney-type
features, warm family fare; occasionally slapstick comedy.

PG—Parental guidance suggested. May contain some pro-
fanities, vulgarities, or a quick nude shot; may include question-
able subject matter or moral views. Since most movie producers
regard a G rating as the kiss of death for box office receipts, a
few swear words or nude shots may be deliberately inserted
into an otherwise "clean" movie in order to attain a PG rating
and thus attract adults.

PG-13—Strong parental guidance suggested for children under the age of thirteen. Some material may be inappropriate for
young children. PG-13 does not, however, require that such
kids be accompanied by an adult, and in truth, it's hard to see
much of a difference between this category and the R rating.
(One upset mother characterized the PG-13 rating as "pretty
gory.")

R—Restricted to those over seventeen years of age, unless accompanied by parent or guardian. An R for violence may include graphic bloodletting scenes, stabbings, eye-gougings, sad-
ism. An R for sex can show frontal nudity, acts of simulated
intercourse, either heterosexual or homosexual. Themes may be
quite provocative. An R rating can also be given for extreme vul-
garity or profanity. R movies occasionally contain all of these ingredients.

X—Restricted to those over age seventeen. Mostly pornogra-
phy; also some noncommercial and foreign films. Theaters must

display an X for unrated imports.

Theater managers are supposed to enforce these attendance codes, but they don't always do so. One recent spot-check in a midwestern suburban community found that only two of the ten theaters asked for identification from teens buying tickets for R-rated films; the rest admitted the kids even though no adult accompanied them.

Even worse are video rental stores; few check IDs to determine whether renters of R-rated films are under age, and in some communities, high-schoolers are permitted to check R-rated movies out of the public library without parental knowledge or consent.

Surveys show that adolescents with home video systems watch more R-rated movies overall (as well as more TV in general) than counterparts without VCRs. And parents seem to be less selective about what their kids watch in homes that have cable and home video systems. While you cannot control what your offspring view in their friends' homes (and home video systems are truly a wonderful invention), it may be worthwhile to set limits on cable or at least not subscribe to certain channels (what sort of message are you sending if you install a "lock box" on the TV, so you can view salient material but Teen can't?).

The point is obvious: we cannot depend on others to do our job. If we object to our teens seeing R-rated movies, then we have to prohibit them from doing so until they are seventeen. This may be an impossible task, but we can at least make the kids aware of our feelings, and help to clarify theirs. But try to have the flexibility to recognize that for a mature teen an occasional R movie might be legitimately instructive—perhaps one that depicts the obscene violence of war. When discussing the issue of movies, ask your teen such questions as:

• How do violent movies make you feel inside? Do you think these feelings are good for you? Can movies be scary and exciting without being excessively bloody, sickening, or degrading?

• How is love portrayed? Who is the hero? How is the premise solved?

• If there's "nothing wrong" with an explicitly sexual film, how would you feel if your little sister saw one? Can you see any connection between the increase in these kinds of films and the increase in rape and other crimes against women? Where would you draw the line? What should and shouldn't be shown in movies? On TV? Why? Will you gain something valuable or become a better person because you saw this film?

Watch your teen carefully. An occasional episode of curiosity involving lewd magazines or films is normal. But if Fourteen is regularly reading pornographic material or sneaking into sexually explicit movies, he's sending out a signal that he needs more information, discussion, or help in dealing with these matters. Don't leave his moral development to others; no matter how awkward you may feel, try to give him what he needs.

Freshman year—laughter, noise; excitement, experiments. Your teen won't tell you everything, but more often than not he *is* willing to listen, debate, question, and discuss. Make the most of this transitional year—it's so very special and so very important.

Chapter 3

Sophomore: The Vulnerable Year

> *The imagination of a boy is healthy, and the imagination of a man is healthy. But there is a space of life in between, in which the soul is in ferment, the character undecided, the way of life uncertain, the ambition thicksighted.*
>
> John Keats, 1818

Sophomore—it comes from the Greek words meaning "wise" and "foolish," and that pretty well sums up the emotional state of the second-year high school student. While Freshman was exuberant, anxious, and scattered, Sophomore is starting to calm down. Now and then, he goes too far in the opposite direction.

A sophomore is *wise* in that he is learning more about himself, developing insights into why he does certain things, why he feels a particular way. He is *foolish* because sometimes he doesn't like what he is learning! He is dissatisfied with himself, and because he's too young to have achieved a sense of perspective, he sees himself forever locked into this lifestyle, this personality, this set of circumstances.

Sophomore year is limiting. Fifteen is still an underclassman with few school privileges or potential for recognition. He's too young for a decent job, which would give him a sense of achievement and the chance to make more of his own spending decisions. He's too young for a driver's license which could provide some freedom. In a sense he's marking time until he gets a bit older. Half of him longs to rebel, to cut loose and make something happen. The other half sinks to apathy: "What's the use? Why bother?"

Many counselors call sophomore year the "vulnerable age," and it seems to be an apt description. Once again your teenager rides a roller coaster, as he did in junior high school, but on this trip the lows are a lot lower than the highs are high. Never again will your child be quite as sensitive to rejection as he is now. A year or two down the road will find him more balanced, more aware and accepting of his potential, more enthusiastic about the future. But today, life seems to have lost its sparkle. There is only the endless, eternal, and utterly depressing Now.

The vulnerable age varies in intensity and length, depending on the sensitivity of the student. "Sometimes it doesn't occur until junior year, or sometimes a kid is very secure at home and vulnerable only at school (or vice versa)," says a counselor. "It's a time when they confess pain, share feelings of inadequacy and uselessness, although sometimes it's hard to talk to parents about these things. This phase may not last a particularly long time either, but it is a super-sensitive time for almost everyone."

Observes a parent, "A century ago kids of this age would have already finished school, and they'd be out working, taking care of themselves and developing responsibility. But our culture keeps kids in a dependent position for a long time. A fifteen-year-old longs to get on with life, and yet his choices are still limited."

There is a positive side to Sophomore's twin image, however. Because he *is* stuck in a holding pattern, he has the luxury of time. He can utilize those free hours to investigate and solidify interests that he may not be able to take advantage of later.

Sophomore year is often the period when extra-curricular school and church activities are at their peak; after spending his first year trying out various sports and clubs, Fifteen finds one or two that whet his interest, and zeroes in on them. Many boys develop a real excitement over cars; they tinker endlessly and have detailed discussions over the model they will buy when they earn their first million. Girls interested in sports refine their techniques, and practice constantly in preparation for varsity try-outs. Both sexes discover satisfying outlets in school clubs or community organizations.

Many teachers regard second year as the golden age in the classroom, too. Sophomores have lost the anxiety that permeated their first year, but haven't yet developed the pseudosophisticated veneer of the upperclassman. They can be lots of fun to teach because they want to know so much and will work hard to achieve their goals.

In addition, Fifteen has probably now found his place with a group of reliable pals, and can spend plenty of time with them. Later, as his schedule gets fuller, he'll have to forfeit some of these pleasures, but for now they provide a real learning experience and take the edge off the vulnerable year.

The child who is happily involved in school, ironically, may be mopey at home. So be good to your sophomore. He needs patience, reassurance, and time.

PHYSICAL CHANGES IN BOYS

One of the bright spots in a fifteen-year-old boy's life usually occurs during sophomore year or just prior to it: he starts to grow. This "shooting up" phase can be dramatic—some boys start second year as children and end it as men (physically, that is; mental and emotional maturity is still a long way off). Arm and leg bones lengthen almost overnight; chest, shoulders, and arm muscles become well-defined. Genitalia enlarge, and Fifteen experiences nocturnal emissions or "wet dreams" on a more persistent basis. Pubic, underarm, and leg hair grows and darkens; some boys sprout chest hair and shave regularly, but most won't add these finishing touches until a year or two later. Fifteen's voice is settling comfortably into the lower register; he has traded his baby fat for a leaner physique and by the end of sophomore year he will have achieved over 90% of his adult height. What a relief! Mom and Dad were right—he isn't going to stay little forever.

While a boy won't hang out in front of a mirror as constantly as his sister, he does spend a lot of time combing his hair, flexing his biceps, and getting acquainted with the sharp dude he is becoming. And to some extent, his self-image is tied up with the way he looks.

"We say good-bye to the worried, hesitant little freshman boys in June," says a teacher, "and over the summer they shoot up. They come back a foot taller, their self-image is more manly, and except for periods of extreme stress, they wouldn't be caught dead expressing their concern over anything."

Sophomore year is the big cover-up for many boys," explains another. "The mirror tells him he's a man, yet inside he feels uncertain, wary, scared of life. How does he reconcile his outward image with the inner turmoil? He covers up, of course, by acting aloof, casual, and oh, so cool."

ACNE

While Teen gets acquainted with his new body image, he also copes with a difficult problem shared by many of his peers: acne. Parents tend to brush acne aside as a minor and temporary nuisance, but to a self-conscious and vulnerable teen, it can be devastating. Acne begins earlier in girls, because of the earlier onset of puberty. By fifteen, just about everyone experiences it to some degree.

Acne is a skin condition in which inflammation and infection of the sebaceous (oil) glands result in pimples, blackheads and cysts, most often on the face, shoulders and back. Teenage skin pores are still tiny and sometimes clog up with dirt or makeup. Then puberty unleashes hormones which, in turn, stimulate the output of the sebaceous glands. Excess oil accumulates under the skin and forms pimples.

In most cases acne is transitory and diminishes when hormones stabilize, in early adulthood. In its mild form it can be controlled by a regular routine of skin cleanliness, using medicated and/or abrasive soap and avoiding heavy makeup. Sunlight also seems to help. Teens should be told *not* to squeeze pimples or irritate skin. More persistent acne can be treated with a variety of oral antibiotics, which can be prescribed by Teen's regular physician. If the case is stubborn, a dermatologist should be consulted. His office procedures may prevent severe disfigurement and future scarring.

Foods such as chocolate, colas, and fried potatoes used to be blamed for acne, but doctors are discovering that their influence is minimal. More important is heredity: the tendency toward oily skin is inherited. It can be controlled, but not eliminated. Many dermatologist believe that stress and pressure also contribute to skin eruptions. One can easily see why the tense, moody sophomore is an obvious candidate for flare-ups. Treatment of acne requires patience and persistence, but much can be done today to improve a teen's appearance so that psychological and social problems are avoided. Help your teen through this awkward time by reassuring him and obtaining proper care.

FIFTEEN AT HOME

Fifteen's aloof, detached attitude will be felt most dramatically at home, especially with sons. Your sophomore may be willing to talk in depth to one special friend or a favorite teacher or even an older sibling, but he rarely communicates meaningfully with Mom or Dad. He drags in after school, omitting a greeting to anyone, and lethargically assembles a snack. He answers questions in quiet monosyllables or with a shrug. Wearily he climbs the stairs to his room (where a KEEP OUT sign is posted on the door) and lies on the bed listening to the same song over and over again. Remember—this may be the same boy who is the life of the party in class!

Sophomore boys aren't usually openly hostile to parents. It seems to be too much trouble. But they do nurse grudges and they can be masters of the sarcastic remark. If pushed into a corner Fifteen can and will react loudly, but right now he'd rather withdraw than fight. Most Fifteens act like this, but it *is* rare for a sophomore boy to weep. If yours does, especially often, it's a tip-off that inner turmoil is somehow getting the best of him, and he's going to need some help. If he can' t or won't open up to you, encourage him to talk to a favorite adult or teacher. If he can't or won't, consider professional counseling, for him or for the whole family. You don't want to let this depression take hold. Time will probably solve most of the problem, but a teenager of any age who cries regularly, who experiences sleep problems, who suddenly fails in school, or who is extremely aggressive, hostile, or anxious, needs help before his feelings bring him to tragedy.

Sophomore girls, also somewhat moody at home, seem to have an easier time venting their "blahs." They slouch around, shoulders sagging, sighing wistfully. But they also manage to verbalize their feelings well. They can be quite argumentative about the pickiest of details, sometimes engaging in a shouting match; then moments later, they dissolve in tears. Mother, of course, doesn't understand. She is trying to ruin Daughter's social life (by insisting that she return home before dawn). In fact, Mother usually becomes the scapegoat for most of Fifteen's misadventures. These clashes are reminiscent of those which took place in junior high but, mercifully, they aren't as intense. Fifteen is maturing, and she now finds it possible to examine her own behavior more honestly and to accept another point of view, occasionally. While Junior High rebelled for the sake of rebellion, Sophomore usually has a reason for the way she feels.

Fifteen seeks liberation, yet she still finds many roads closed to her because of her age. So she compromises by pulling away from her family, manifested in sparse conversation, a locked bedroom door, or meals eaten separately. Some Fifteens go further and refuse to get involved in family outings or even in holiday celebrations at home. This attitude is apt to hurt parents, especially if the family has heretofore enjoyed vacations or holidays together. Is Fifteen turning into a hermit? Doesn't she care about Grandpa anymore? How can we have a warm Christmas morning around the tree, if she won't even get out of bed?

Parents can, of course, insist that Fifteen join the group. But her sullen, pouty face is definitely going to steal luster from the occasion, and add to Mom and Dad's irritation as well. Another solution might be to leave the choice of involvement up to Teen, except for a few "must" appearances. Pressure to appear often propels her in the opposite direction and removing that pressure relieves tension for other family members. It also gives Teen some control over her life. Let your teen know she is welcome at family functions and encourage her to attend. But don't make her feel guilty if she'd rather do something else. If Fifteen's previous relationships with her family have been rewarding, she'll return to them when the time is right.

Despite their aloofness, sophomores still need physical affection from their parents. Boys are *not* too big to be hugged, and even though Fifteen may duck his mother's embrace, he understands the gesture and is pleased by it. Unfortunately, some fathers avoid touching their sons once they've grown tall, believing that hugging isn't quite okay between them anymore, and that Son should "start acting like a real man," which presumably means shelving his softer, more tender feelings. Such an attitude is a mistake. Physical affection never made a sissy out of any male, and touch can be a powerful communication tool between men, who often don't easily verbalize their feelings. A father-to-son pat on the back, hand on the shoulder, or affectionate bear-hug all say, "I care about you. I understand." Boys need this message.

Our culture is more positive about parents hugging daughters, but the female Fifteen can be just as squirrely and withdrawn as her brother, at times. However, that's no reason to abandon the practice. Girls especially value closeness with their fathers. "They need gratification, affection, dignity, tenderness," says a teacher. "If I were the father of a fifteen-year-old girl, I'd make sure I was giving her plenty of love—so she wouldn't look for it from an older boy instead."

Sometimes families just aren't physically affectionate. If this is the case, verbal endearments can substitute. The vulnerable sophomore needs reassurance that she is okay, that she is going in the right direction. "You look beautiful tonight." "You did a fine job." "I'm proud of you." Such warm remarks may have no outwardly visible effect on the moody sophomore, but inside, where it really matters, she's hearing the language of love.

CURFEWS

Love, of course, must be coupled with discipline, especially with Fifteen eager to test her wings and break out of the restrictions of childhood. One of the most typical battles with sophomores is over the matter of curfews. "I'm older now," Fifteen points out. "Why can't I go out on school nights? And why do I have to be in so early?"

Good parents realize that they must encourage healthy independence. But how much leeway should Fifteen be given in the matter of curfews?

Fortunately, many communities have already established legal curfews for minors, and police will stop a child who is out after hours. These community rules provide a framework within which parents can work to establish their own rules. Your local police force can advise you of the law in your area.

Many townships have established guidelines for nighttime behavior, similar to the following. These may help you in instructing your teen:

1. Teens should be discouraged from going out on school nights unless they are attending a school or community function or studying at the library—in short, something with a purpose to it. They should return home, walking in a group, or be picked up by a parental carpool at the conclusion of the event. Older teens may be permitted to work on school nights, but job hours should be kept to a minimum so as not to interfere with class work.

2. Teens should be discouraged from "hanging out" or driving around with no particular destination in mind, since undesirable situations can easily develop.

3. Weekend curfews can be extended, particularly for parties, school sporting events, dances, and dating. Parents should always know where their teens are going, who they are with, and how they are getting home.

If your teenager refuses to give you this information, or deliberately gives you false information, then she is displaying juvenile, untrustworthy behavior and obviously is not ready for adult privileges. Impress upon your teen that with every *right* there is a corresponding *responsibility* ; if she has the right to be out of the house at night, she also has the duty to advise you honestly of her whereabouts.

One mistake that parents sometimes make is to set an arbitrary curfew ("11:30 sharp!") and then ground Teen automatically if she is even five minutes late. Such a rule is unreasonable, and can set up a needlessly hostile situation between parent and teen. It can also lead to lying, when Teen tries to think up a good reason why she was late, in order to avoid the penalty. We adults can't always predict exactly when *we* will be home after an evening out. All sorts of complications can occur. So why should we demand such hard-and-fast actions from our offspring?

A better way to handle curfews is to talk over the "who, what, and where" information with Teen, and then ask her what time she thinks she will be home. This approach gives the teenager some input in the decisionmaking process and a feeling of control, which she really wants and needs. If she names a reasonable time, the parent agrees, providing the daughter phones if plans change and she will be home later than originally agreed. If she does not phone and gets home well past curfew, not just a few minutes ... If she phones, is granted a short extension, and abuses the privilege by coming in quite late ... If she comes in on time but it's later discovered that she was not where she was supposed to be ... she has forfeited the right to determine her own curfew. Mom and Dad will have to do it for her for an extended period, until she can regain their trust. Sometimes there are extenuating circumstances, and parents must judge each case on its own merits. But rather than a power struggle, the goal of curfew decisions should be mutual trust and respect. As one mother puts it, "I raised five teenagers and rarely had a curfew problem. The kids felt relaxed and happy on their dates because they knew I trusted them and wouldn't overreact if they were a little late sometimes. And I didn't have to pace the floor because I could count on them to keep me informed."

Even if kids do respect curfew rules, there are going to be times when parents refuse permission for certain events. Is a freshman girl mature enough to be taken to the senior prom? Should kids be allowed to attend a rock concert? Is the driver responsible? Will the party be unchaperoned? It's difficult to restrict a teen whose conduct has been exemplary, but our children deserve protection. We have to care enough to provide it, despite the inevitable storm clouds. When these situations occur, be sure your teen knows that you trust *her*, but you do not trust the *situation*—and that's why you can't permit her to go. She will be angry but she also may be silently relieved. Perhaps she senses that the event would be too much for her to handle, but doesn't yet have the courage to say "no" to her peers.

DRUGS

One of the most pervasive and difficult problems for parents to handle is the rising use of drugs among teenagers. Most parents of teenagers were teens themselves at a time when drug use was uncommon. Although our generation experimented with cigarettes and alcohol, we rarely did so in junior high, nor did we become habitual users at a tender age. But today our teens function within a commercialized youth culture which often takes teenage drug use for granted. Popular music speaks glowingly of "getting high"; drugs are sold and used openly at rock concerts; movies and TV shows occasionally seem to treat drug use sympathetically. Even worse is the confusing legal status of marijuana or pot, the most popular of today's drugs. In the 1960s, as pot became popular at universities, criminal charges were often brought against casual users. Since penalties were harsh, a public movement began to revise the marijuana laws. Now marijuana laws for adults vary widely from state to state; in many places limited pot use is regarded as benign, and no attempt is even made to enforce existing laws. Pot is always illegal for minors, but kids can often interpret lax adult restrictions as a sign of society's tolerance for youth use.

Drugs are easy to obtain. The idea of a sinister drug pusher who lurks around school yards in a big black car is largely mythical. Kids get drugs from their own friends or from older teens who have connections. Often a "smoke" is as close as the local teen hangout, forest preserve, or school bathroom.

Pot and other drugs can be extremely harmful to a young, growing body. According to the U.S. Department of Health and Human Services:

1. The effects of marijuana vary with potency. There are over 350 chemicals in pot. THC is the major mood-altering chemical, but at least three others interact with THC. The amounts of these chemicals vary with each mixture of pot, and thus can produce different effects. (In this respect, marijuana differs from alcohol, which has controlled ingredients.) The effect also depends on body weight, which means that young users may be getting a double dose merely by using the same amount as adults. Although pot is supposed to be relaxing, young users are susceptible to acute panic reactions, nausea, tremors, and fainting.

2. The active ingredients in marijuana accumulate in the body. A week after a person has smoked a marijuana cigarette, 30 to 50% of THC remains in the body and brain. If use is regular, one's system is never free of the drug. (Here again, marijuana contrasts with alcohol, which is usually washed out of the system within 24 hours.)

Scientists aren't sure how the accumulation of these chemicals affects the body, but they worry that this slow, subtle build-up may cause permanent personality and behavioral changes.

3. Heavy use of marijuana decreases the level of sex hormones, a real risk to teenagers, since a healthy hormonal balance is crucial for normal physical and emotional development in young people. Like cigarettes, pot can damage lung and bronchial tissue and have adverse effects on the heart. It also interferes with motor functions, such as those needed to drive a car.

Perhaps even more disturbing than these physical consequences are the drug's effects on a teen's personality. An effective public service TV ad shows a machine graphing actively-moving brain waves, while the narrator states, "This is the brain activity of a normal fourteen-year-old." The next picture is one of an almost-flat wave, accompanied by the chilling message: "This is the brain wave of a fourteen-year-old who has just smoked pot." Research bears it out. Young users do tend to become apathetic and lethargic, losing interest in vigorous wholesome pursuits, their lives narrowing in focus. Apathy alternates with unpredictable hostile flare-ups and a tendency toward paranoia may arise.

4. Heavy users develop a tolerance to pot. Although not classified as an addictive drug like heroin and the barbiturates, recent studies show that long-time users increase their dosage to satisfy higher tolerance levels. Marijuana can also be a "gateway" into other drugs. The National Institute on Drug Abuse points out that if people do not use marijuana and alcohol, they simply do not use other illegal substances. Although the majority of teen pot smokers will not go on to other drugs, heavy users proceed to:

• Pills (stimulants, sedatives and tranquilizers), often used in combinations) or inhalants such as glue, aerosol propellants or nitrous oxide (used in dentists' offices as an anesthetic and called "laughing gas").

• Hallucinogens or psychedelics, such as LSD, mescaline, peyote, cocaine, or PCP (angel dust). Of all these substances, cocaine is probably the fastest-growing in popularity, and available now to all age groups. Just a tiny amount produces an enormous high, followed quickly by depression, anxiety, confusion and in some cases, manic-depressive illnesses. Deaths from co-caine-induced heart attacks have risen rapidly in recent years.

• Crack, now apparently the drug of choice among adoles-cents. Composed of cocaine mixed with baking soda and water, crack is five to ten times more powerful than "coke" although of shorter duration, and appears to be far more deadly and addic-tive than any drugs previously used in abundance by teens.

We parents cannot afford to underestimate the serious ef-fects of drug use. What started several years ago among a minor counterculture on college campuses is now common in grade school. By sophomore year, almost every teen will have been exposed to drugs, by being offered them at parties or at school or by observing classmates who are "stoned." Our kids will be forced to make decisions about drug use again and again.

Why, given all the negative repercussions, do so many youngsters get involved with drugs? For some, it's simply an experiment, another way of finding out about the world. They may smoke part of a joint once or twice, satisfy their curiosity, and be done with it. Others try drugs for the same reason that they wear certain fashions or use certain slang—because it seems "cool" and some of their friends do it. Studies indicate that the number of peers who use drugs is the major influence on a youngster's decision to use them. Furthermore, a drug-using child tends to limit her friends to other drug users, leading to a circular pattern of reinforcement. The "birds of a feather" phi-losophy is definitely true here; if your child hangs out with pals who use pot or other drugs, he probably does too or is at least seriously considering it.

Kids are also affected by what they see adults do. And since Mom and Dad live in a drug-oriented, pleasure-seeking society too, we often try to avoid pain. Got a headache? Reach for the aspirin. Nervous? Try a tranquilizer. Need to relax after a hard day at the office? Break out the cocktails. Because drugs are of-ten regarded by adults as instant cures, our kids come to view them as problem solvers.

Finally, drugs do indeed relieve pain, at least temporarily, and adolescence can be a hurtful period. Teens are anxious about their bodies, their social lives, their grades, their relation-ships with parents. There is no doubt that drugs bring a brief respite from these uncomfortable feelings.

As parents, we know that life's problems can be met without using drugs. If booze and pills are used as crutches, a teen may never learn how to handle boredom, disappointment and loneliness in a normal way; her emotional development will be arrested at child-level, as she avoids the opportunity to mature. Our challenge is to develop self-reliant, confident kids who like and accept themselves, and feel no need to wrap themselves in the drug culture. And this effort, of course, begins at birth. But even the most loving and well-meaning parent may one day discover that her teen is experimenting with drugs. If this happens, what should our reaction be?

Like a lot of other habits, drug use usually starts slowly, and parents go through stages of awareness just like our teen. The first is ignorance. Parents begin to notice personality changes—hostility, sneakiness—but attribute them to the normal teen reticence (which they may certainly be, if other symptoms do not accompany them).

The next parental step is denial. Warning signs such as a teen's red eyes (from smoking marijuana) or incense burning in his room to cover the scent, secretiveness about friends, breaking house rules, money missing from around the house, cutting classes at school—all of these can be signs of teen drug use, but parents are often afraid to confront the situation openly. "You'd be amazed how many will say, 'Not my child!' when we call after finding a bag of marijuana on their kid," says a high school psychologist. "But drugs must be confronted openly, because they aren't going to go away by themselves."

Next comes an attempt to minimize—"Well, it's only pot; thank God he isn't into the 'hard stuff'" is one way of trying to make ourselves feel better about a situation we think we can't control. But as many battle-scarred parents can testify, there's not much here to be grateful about; pot, as we've seen, is often just the beginning of the nightmare.

Eventually, when drug use has become the most dominant part of a family's life, when it takes over the household and most decisions or activities seem to revolve around it, many adults finally realize that something must be done. Unfortunately, there may be little, at this stage, that will be effective.

Rather than staggering through such a heartbreaking scenario, try some prevention. For one thing, spend more time with your youngster and get to know his friends and their parents. Ask him about drug use. If he denies it but unusual behavior remains, intensify your investigation. "There are no sure proofs of drug use except actually finding the drug," says a youth officer. That's why, although searching a teen's room is usually a breach of trust, it's a prudent thing to do if drug use is strongly suspected. If you find evidence—such as a marijuana smell (a sweet odor), a marijuana butt, leaves, powder, rolling papers, alcohol bottles, pills, eyedrop bottles, or room deodorizers—take immediate action.

1. Confront your teenager when you and she are both in control. Hysterical outbursts or angry accusations, especially if directed at a stoned teenager, are ineffective. But a firm, no-nonsense approach can work. Let her know that drug use will not be tolerated. Period. Your child cannot be allowed to jeopardize her healthy growth by substance abuse.

2. Back up your no-drug statement with clear, consistent rules and be willing to enforce them. It's difficult for a teen to live in a loose, shifting environment. Most drug-troubled teens complain that their parents are hypocritical, aloof or uncaring. Few complain about strictness. It's important to establish a fair and effective punishment, and use it each time your youngster gets out of line. This may take months, but your seriousness will mean a lot to even the most drug-troubled child. If she has been using substances in an attempt to make you take notice of her and demonstrate your care, she will actually be grateful for your strong stand.

If peer pressure is part of the problem (and it usually is), grounding a teenager and taking away telephone privileges are sensible. This extracts Teen from the group with which she may be trying drugs and gives her a chance to clear her body and mind of their effect. Curfew rules will have to be reevaluated in light of this breach of trust; you may also want to bar Teen's friends from visits. One punishment that usually brings an immediate response is taking away Teen's electronic appliances: hair dryers, curlers, stereos, TVs, video games, and the like.

Throughout this period your attitude should be decent, but ultra-firm. Name-calling, brow-beating, and other personally humiliating tactics will only compound the problem of teen rebellion. Instead, let your child know that you are hurt and disappointed in her, but that you care enough not to let her damage herself. Encourage her to talk about why she got involved; listen for messages of pain, inadequacy, helplessness that may be hidden underneath her words. Ask questions, and work out new ways of behavior together.

3. Enlist the aid of other parents. Parent power begins at home, but it's most effective when it includes a network. The teen's strategy of "divide and conquer" no longer works if a community of adults all feel the same way. Unfortunately, many parents are either ashamed to admit a teen drug problem to others, or they refuse to believe that their child could be involved. Parental support doesn't have to wait until a crisis, however; parents can simply invite neighbors and parents of their children's peers over for an evening of general discussion about their teens' activities. *Toughlove* is one national organization which has worked successfully in this way in many communities. Members communicate by attending weekly meetings in each other's homes. They discuss rules of behavior, give each other permission to call the police if neighborhood activities are getting out of hand, discuss proper party guidelines and develop alternative opportunities for healthy teen activities. By providing a united front, they defuse the "everybody's doing it" argument, and make it easier for a group of teens to function within generally accepted guidelines.

A typical parent network might begin with a statement of support, perhaps circulated throughout the neighborhood or sent from school, such as the following:

"Because we are concerned about adolescent and preteen use of drugs and alcohol, and

Because we believe that our kids need support to feel comfortable when they choose not to use alcohol or other drugs, and

Because we believe that parents need the help of one another to make life safer for all our children

We agree: to encourage healthy, chaperoned activities for our youngsters, to not allow alcoholic beverages or any other drug to be consumed by minors on our premises, and to freely contact one another when in doubt about an activity."

Such a contract can be signed, a list of signers compiled and circulated among one another and the contract posted in a prominent place (perhaps the refrigerator) so Teen gets the message: Mom and Dad are not alone!

4. Check out the resources at school. Many high schools have counselors, psychologists and drug experts who will be happy to talk with your teenager and/or refer him to community help. Once he is off drugs, school counselors try to introduce him to activities which can bring him pleasure and a "natural high," such as biking, cross-country skiing, community service. The knowledge that adults outside the family care can mean a great deal to a troubled teen; often he will open up more readily to these nonjudgmental folks than to his parents. Counseling does not take the place of parental involvement, but it can be a good supplement.

It is interesting to note that households characterizing themselves as "involved in religious life" have fewer offspring embroiled in the drug culture than those who do not. When drug-free kids are asked why they have chosen this lifestyle, many put it in spiritual terms: "Because I believe it would be displeasing to God" or "God made my body, and I want to keep it healthy for him."

Ironically, it is rare for God to be mentioned in any discussion about preventing drug involvement. *And yet the mention of Him saturates the literature on treatment.* The first three steps addicted people must take in organizations such as Alcoholics Anonymous or Addicts Anonymous are to state that they cannot handle the problem alone, acknowledge that God (or a Higher Power) can handle it, and allow this Higher Power to take control of their lives.

While adolescents often rebel against organized religion or church attendance, and while religion by itself is not a panacea against trouble, many kids benefit by believing that Someone out there cares about every aspect of their lives, and loves them unconditionally. The home is a better place for a youngster to be introduced to God than a drug treatment center. Think about your own beliefs, and see if you can share them with Teen.

5. If, however, your youngster's drug use cannot be stopped, you should contact a local drug treatment center, which can be done with the help of your child's physician. It may be necessary to place Teen under the care of medical personnel, either on an outpatient basis or admitting her, if the problem is acute.

This can be a drastic step, but also a life-saving one. The welfare of your child is at stake. And if you don't act, who will?

RUNAWAYS

As we've seen, the sophomore longs for independence and feels that it will never come, even though she judges herself ready to handle it. If she is also living in a troubled home situation, she may believe that her only option is to leave. Over a million teenagers choose this solution each year, and the "average runaway" is a fifteen-year-old girl.

Runaways fall into two loose groups—those who leave home without parental consent, and those who are literally thrown out because their parent can't or won't care for them anymore. This second group—the "throwaways"—have usually been in trouble for a long time. They may have been sexually or physically abused at home by parents, step-parents, or siblings; they feel emotionally abandoned and rejected; and they usually have a history of unstable, anti-social behavior at school or in the community. For them, leaving home is not an adventurous lark. They are fleeing from what they consider to be an intolerable situation. With no skills, schooling, or money, they nonetheless board buses or hitchhike into big cities, where they feel certain they can start a new life on their own.

Instead they often fall prey to pimps or child pornographers who pick them up, offer food, lodging, and love, then use them, abuse them, and often murder them. Those who do manage to find a safe shelter, such as Covenant House in New York's infamous Eighth Avenue sin strip, often decide to call home, only to discover that in many cases, their parents refuse to let them come back. Says Reverend Bruce Ritter, founder of Covenant House, "Of the more than 5000 kids who came to us in the past twenty months, we could only send 1000 home." Father Ritter and his staff try to persuade the remaining throwaways to leave their destructive lifestyle, give up drugs and prostitution, enroll in school, and start again in a new direction. "But in too many cases the damage has been massive; almost 70% of our youngsters go back to the streets," says the priest. "They simply don't believe that they can survive any other way, or that they deserve a life free of degradation."

The majority of runaways fall into the first category, however, and don't represent such a hopeless lot. They too have problems; in fact, "not getting along with my parents" is usually cited as their primary reason for running away. But most of this group travels no farther than ten miles from home; sometimes they just hide out at a friend's house for a night or two. When they are located, their parents usually respond to the situation. "After all," says one counselor, "the parents are probably hurting just as much as the kids."

To deal with the problems of runaways, a nationwide network of runaway shelter houses, drop-in centers, hot-lines, and group homes has sprung into existence. They are advertised heavily at city bus stations and other locations where runaway teenagers may land. These newer organizations differ from existing social service agencies in that they do not regard their teen clientele as delinquent or mentally disturbed. They see family conflicts as potential growth opportunities, they offer counseling and privacy rather than punishment, and they try to get the parent involved as soon as possible. Most won't contact parents, however, without the teen's consent. Since the majority of runaways don't leave their own locales, counseling therefore can be offered within the community—as a benefit to everyone. If your youngster does run away, check first with her friends and their parents. Alert any community runaway shelters and call the police (although police don't often locate runaways). National toll-free telephone hot-lines will also take your message and relay it to your child if she calls in from any part of the country.

Usually within a few days your child will be back at home. She may be chastened, somewhat frightened, but she may still be defiant too. Be sure to start family counseling right away. Running away is almost always a cry for help, and all of you must face these needs and learn to deal with them.

Every sophomore wants desperately to become a "somebody." This natural process develops in steps. One of the first steps is the struggle to achieve healthy independence. This effort is not the same as rebellion; it becomes rebellion only when the quest for independence overreaches itself. Parents help teens by giving them the chance to make decisions within a supportive set of guidelines.

Try to recognize and accept your sophomore's temporary frustrations amidst his need to take charge of himself. Reassure him that, despite his fears, life will eventually change for the better. Treat him with politeness, hug him frequently, leave a love-note on his pillow, saying something like, "I care. I'm here if you want to talk." Then stay out of his way. At this point, Fifteen is his own worst enemy. But better days are coming.

Chapter 4

Junior:
The Year of Integration

Give me those days with heart in riot, The depths of
bliss that touch on pain, The force of hate, and love's
disquiet—Ah, give me back my youth again!
Goethe

The third year of high school, and a new beginning. The sixteen-year-old has partially broken out of her cocoon of insecurity, restlessness, and indecision. She is emerging as a stronger, more satisfied individual. Much growth still lies ahead, but from time to time parents are apt to catch a glimpse of the adult their teen will become one day. Change comes slowly—two steps forward, one step back—but it is definitely happening.

Junior year is sometimes characterized as a year of *integration*, when a variety of elements, once pulling in different directions, now start to come together in a harmonious pattern. How do these signs of integration begin to appear?

INTEGRATING PARTS INTO A WHOLE

• If when younger, your teen was allowed to rebel or define herself in non-harmful ways—messy bedrooms, strange clothing fads, loud music—she has probably fulfilled this psychological need and feels a lot calmer about it now. However, if she has *not* been permitted to "make her statement," prepare for fireworks. This stage cannot be skipped and a junior will fight hard to establish her identity. Many of the issues Junior used to argue about, just for the sake of arguing, have dwindled in importance

She is no longer interested in battling at every opportunity. But don't be lulled into a sense of security—there are still problems to be addressed and handled. However, Sixteen is more reasonable now, and she welcomes a rational dialogue even if she doesn't always get her way. But her bedroom will still be messy.

• If you have been firm and consistent in the guidelines you've set, but also willing to understand your teen's point of view, some of your efforts may now be paying off. For Sixteen takes a tentative step back into the family structure, but no longer as a child. She has struggled to gain some independence, to become separate from her family, and she is not about to relinquish the strides she has made. But she does want to interact more closely with Mom and Dad—*if* they can view her as a grownup rather than a child. Teens of this age are much more accepting of Dad as he *is*. They have lost their childhood hero-worship permanently. They have worked through some anger at what they perceived as Dad's overprotectiveness, or even disinterest. They are now coming to terms with a more realistic assessment of their father, warts and all. Sometimes they can even air conflicting principles with Dad, without worrying too much about repercussions. How close father and offspring eventually become depends a great deal on how willing Dad is to "open up," to share his own feelings, to talk matters over in a candid and kindred spirit, rather than lecturing or giving orders. But even if the father-teenager relationship is less than ideal (and most still are, at this stage), juniors seem to see their male parent more clearly, and to accept his limitations more readily. Girls may even return to displays of affection for Dad, dropping their previous "too-cool-to-care" attitude.

Such pleasantness extends to Mom, too, at least from her sons. Sixteen, now more confident of his male image, finds himself on friendlier terms with his mother; he talks to her as an equal, assuming that she will treat him the same way. Sometimes he even discusses problems with her, although they are rarely of a personal nature. He acts as protector, volunteering to carry heavy items for her, telling her how nice she looks. Mother-daughter relationships still have a way to go, however, especially now that new conflicts over dating and partying will have to be faced. But occasionally Mom and Sixteen find themselves sharing a shopping trip, a tennis game, or a late-night conversation with real closeness and warmth. It doesn't happen all the time, but there is a definite improvement in communication.

Things smooth out with younger siblings as well. Sixteen regards herself as an elder statesman of sorts, too grown up to get involved in juvenile high jinx. So it's a wonderful time for parents to enlist her help with younger children, *not* as a disciplinarian but rather as an advisor. You might wish to discuss a problem you're having with a younger child, as long as it's not anything that would violate his privacy. Ask Sixteen for advice. You'll be amazed at the insight she possesses, and she'll be flattered at your confidence in her.

• If throughout her earlier years your teen has been loved unconditionally—that is, valued for what she *is*, not what she can *do*—junior year seems to be the time when she becomes more comfortable with herself. She begins to realize that her too-large nose is really not the end of the world after all; he begins to see that his inability to make the football varsity team has no bearing on his worth as a human being. Sixteens grow in tolerance not only for others, but for themselves too. Life is better now, and they understand that much of it is due to their own attitudes.

"A junior starts to realize that he is not the ugliest person in the world, that he does have many good qualities, that he is likeable and has talent," says a teacher. "He's coming together as a person. By now friends have shared their own insecurities with him, and he realizes that he isn't the only person who ever felt lost or depressed. The teen years are all I-centered, but Sixteen is finally developing a sense of perspective."

One caution—in junior year teens move into a more competitive arena, particularly in terms of sports and grades. And if a teen has previously been pushed by parents to excel in these areas, he's going to be under tremendous pressure now. It's good for parents to be at games, to care and to encourage their young athletes, but if Sixteen gets praise only for his prowess on the football field, he may become a one-dimensional person. If he is praised for grades and gets attention for them, but not for other things, he's going to assume that his value begins and ends with a listing on the honor roll. Especially now, as he is becoming more integrated, *all* sides of Sixteen's personality should be nourished. Watch your teen and try to reinforce the aspects of his personality which you appreciate, but to which you normally pay little attention. Don't overemphasize winning the game or getting all A's at the expense of the other good qualities he's beginning to demonstrate.

• Finally, if your son has been encouraged to talk frankly about issues such as sex, drugs, and religious beliefs, without Mom or Dad having a coronary whenever a controversial subject is aired, he can now start to define his own standards. By bouncing them off others such as parents, teachers, clergy, and peers, he has begun to shape his own ideas. He has listened to differing viewpoints and has begun to sift and sort these impressions into a code of his own. Because he values himself and his uniqueness, he is starting to realize that blindly following the crowd is not always in his best interest. Furthermore, he finds that he can sometimes stand up against the crowd without getting excited and without using his parents as an excuse. The peer group is still tremendously important, but its impact is becoming more socially satisfying and is mind-controlling. Sixteen can and does follow the crowd, but sometimes he's not afraid to lead it in a new direction, too. He's more aware of his own opinions, daring to question and even criticize the group's influence. And this independence is what will sometimes save him from exploits that everyone else seems to be experiencing.

Much of Sixteen's development is taking place on the *inside*. This growth is harder to recognize than the dramatic physical changes of the past, but it is even more valuable. Although self-centered, Sixteen becomes more balanced, self-reliant, cheerful and happy. His mind expands and his emotions relax. Within this framework he will meet many new issues this year. With parental encouragement, he can handle them.

WORKING

Part of the settling that can go on at sixteen stems from the fact that society now officially recognizes his growth. No longer are certain activities barred to him. He can move into the first of a series of grownup privileges with the sanction of the adult community.

One of these rites of passage is the official part-time job. The high school junior is no longer hindered by child labor laws, which prohibit many companies from hiring workers under the age of sixteen. (Legally, kids under sixteen can work, but only at certain jobs and usually only if permit forms have been filled out and approved by school and work-site personnel. And in most cases, under-sixteens aren't permitted to work during the hours when classes are in session or past 7 p.m. except during summer.) With the dawning of that "magic birthday" however, Teen is no longer limited to an occasional babysitting job or morning paper route either. Along with his counterparts (according to the Bureau of Labor, one-half of all sixteen- to nineteen-year-old students have regular employment), his options now abound—usher or candy clerk at the local movie theater, bus boy, department store helper, supermarket bagger, evening typist, and that perennial favorite, short-order cook (70% of fast-food employees are younger than twenty-one). Few adults, steeped in the endless nine-to-five treadmill, can understand Sixteen's eagerness to join the work world. After all, we reason, he'll be earning an income for the rest of his life once school is over. Why get involved so early?

But to a teen, a job represents more than just spending money. It also signifies responsibility, power and increasing control over one's own life and decisions. He's waited so long for this opportunity, and it is a significant step in the growth process.

Along with every step forward, of course, come increased learning experiences—and additional problems, too. One of the first difficulties to surface after a job has been found are the number of hours per week it will involve. Mom and Dad may have envisioned an eight-hour Saturday shift for Teen—comfortable, not too demanding, still leaving plenty of time for homework and extracurricular pursuits. The reality, however, is very different. Most of the places that hire part-time workers, primarily from among the pool of teens and housewives, expect at least a twenty-hour commitment each week; in many cases, even more. Most of these hours can be worked over the weekend, but theaters, fast food chains, stores and supermarkets that are open on weekday evenings (and that includes most of them) expect their young employees to man these nighttime shifts as well. In fact, one of the most common on-the-job problems kids report is being asked to stay later than they anticipated. Frequently, employers will go home, leaving youngsters with the responsibility of closing up at night, a situation few parents feel comfortable about. And yet, even though many areas of the country are experiencing a shortage of young workers, few employers are willing to accommodate the teen who always wants to go home early. Someone has to "close"—and your child will be expected to take his turn.

You should also stay vigilant (although in the background) about other on-the-job problems. For example, because teens are guileless about the work world, they sometimes do not understand the unspoken rules. More than one new worker has been fired from a supermarket or ice cream parlor because he gave pals "free samples" or allowed them a "complimentary" check through the line. If you ask this teen if his behavior would be considered "stealing," he'd have to think a moment before grudgingly saying "yes." That's because giving a pal a pass seems friendly rather than illegal (and remember, he often acts on the spur of the moment). Talk to yours, using a "what do you think would happen" scenario—it may be an eye-opener for both of you.

Naive adolescents can also be taken advantage of by unscrupulous bosses or even victimized by co-workers. One sixteen-year-old girl put up with lewd comments and abusive language from a male teenaged crew leader because, as his "inferior," she believed she had no recourse; a young waiter had the cost of some broken dishes deducted from his paycheck although he claimed he had not been responsible for the damage. Your teen has definite responsibilities to those who employ him, but he also has rights. Be alert to grumblings that seem more than the usual gripe sessions, and if you believe your teen is being exploited, encourage him to phone the local branch of the state or federal department of labor and ask for more information.

Most entry-level jobs for teens pay minimum wage; in areas of the country where young workers are in short supply, starting rates are higher. The typical teenager is impressed with this pay scale until he gets the first check and experiences the shock of deductions for federal, state, and social security withholding taxes and in some cases, union dues and uniform costs. That attractive-sounding salary certainly has dwindled! And while this economics lesson is valuable, it often pushes Teen into working even longer hours in order to make up the difference.

Working hours are one of the areas where parents will have to hold a firm stand, despite pressure. That's because some recent studies are finding that *extensive* part-time employment can take a toll on a youngster's growth and development. For example, work can contribute to classroom fatigue, perhaps even influencing a teacher's effectiveness. ("When you look into a sea of exhausted faces, you often downgrade your expectations," remarked one senior English teacher.) Tired kids do less of the exploring, risk-taking, reflecting and even daydreaming that are part of adolescence; they instead may select easier courses (to keep up averages with less effort), and cut back on extracurricular activities. In one California study, researchers also noted that employed teens copied other people's homework, cheated on tests and skipped school more frequently than peers who were not employed.

Remember that your youngster's first priority right now is *school*, and while a job can offer learning experiences of a different kind, it cannot be allowed to take precedence over the classroom. In addition, as the junior integrates his personality, an important goal is *balance*. He can benefit by the challenge of adding job hours to a schedule that already includes school, homework, outside activities, social events and family reorganizational skills. But if the job takes too much of his time and strength, to the detriment of his primary roles, balance will be sacrificed.

"When our Tim started working at the hamburger stand, we set a maximum of twenty hours for him," his mother reports. "He worked about twelve hours over the weekend, which still left two evening shifts on school nights. We told him that if his grades stayed the same or improved next quarter, he could keep the job. Otherwise, it would have to go. He did manage, and as time went on, he learned to make better use of his time."

"Betty was putting in so much time at work that she considered dropping school band and the tennis team," says another parent. "I felt she needed these outlets, but the store manager refused to cut her hours. Finally Betty quit her job, kept the activities and went back to babysitting. It's been hard on her financially—but we both feel she made the right decision."

As in many areas, each case is different and will have to be decided on its own merits. Most parents recommend allowing Sixteen to start a job, but recommend also keeping a close eye on the lifestyle it promotes. If problems of fatigue, sliding grades and profound lack of organization occur so acutely that they cannot be adjusted, hours on the job should be cut back or eliminated temporarily. Kids develop at different rates, and a girl who can't coordinate school, activities and job in junior year may manage splendidly by the time she is a senior.

Once Teen has a job, the next area of conflict usually involves spending money. Many kids have definite goals in mind—they want to pay auto expenses, save for college, cover dating costs. If parents have gradually moved out of the picture financially, by withdrawing the allowance or buying fewer clothing and luxury items for Teen, most kids automatically pick up the slack, covering their day-to-day school and social expenses, some clothing purchases, and an occasional big-ticket item such as a new stereo. Most teens become educated consumers at this point, making an occasional mistake but usually getting good value for their money. And it's amazing how many now forsake higher-priced designer labels in favor of sale merchandise! Occasionally, especially if a child has not earned *any* money until now, he will assume that what he earns is his, to spend on what frivolity strikes his fancy. He sees no reason to assume any financial responsibility for himself. That's what parents are for! This situation calls for some straightforward discussions, as well as a gradual withdrawal of the allowance. Encourage your teen to save a portion of his income. If he doesn't have a savings account by now, see that he opens one. Help him draw up a budget for his other needs. Be aware that if you allow your child to spend all or nearly all of his earnings on his own whims and desires, you are unwittingly encouraging self-centeredness and materialism, as well as an upscale lifestyle he will hardly be able to afford once he is out from under your economic protection. Instead, emphasize the positive—you are proud that he is shouldering responsibility, making plans for the future, wanting to be his own person. He will need to set goals—like what new clothes he will need this year, what social events he'll have to pay for—and he will have to decide which of these costs he will undertake on his own. Tell him you will supplement his costs; explain exactly how much you will be giving him, but let him know that the rest is up to him.

Then stand back and let him do it! If he agrees to be responsible for his shoe purchases, then later asks you for a pair because he spent all his loot on sports equipment, let him wear the old ones, holes and all. If he promised to buy his own movie tickets, but has no cash tonight and pleads, "It's a great movie! Honest, Ma, I'll pay you back," turn a deaf ear. You do Teen no favor by jumping in and rescuing him from his own mistakes. Eventually, when the shoes get uncomfortable enough, or when he gets tired of missing good movies, he'll find a way to balance his budget, and he'll take a giant step in responsibility at the same time. Just be sure that spending decisions are made *before* the fact and understood clearly by everyone involved.

Part-time jobs and resulting spending decisions can also bring complications into a smoothly running home—odd hours, parental chauffeuring duty, reheated meals. Some parents, especially those who are financially secure, are tempted to avoid the whole scene and simply keep Junior on the dole until he's twenty-one. This can be a mistake, for if we provide *things* for our children instead of values, purposes and challenges to make them grow, we cheat them. When we refuse them the opportunity for difficult experiences in the name of our own comfort, we rob them of a belief in themselves, the chance to meet different situations and learn to handle themselves competently.

If you have spoiled your child by providing her with every material desire, now is the time to draw back and let her accept some responsibility. With this attitude, you are paying tribute to the fact that she is indeed growing up.

DRIVING

Another momentous event occurs during the third year of high school. Sixteen is given official permission to obtain a license to drive a car. This particular situation, so well-defined by law, throws parents into a tailspin for many reasons.

- The accident rate among teenage drivers, especially boys,

is horrifying. Teens speed, defy traffic laws, and often play games with each other on the highway. Some of the resulting smash-ups are simply inconvenient fender-benders, but far too many involve serious injury or even death to drivers, passengers and pedestrians. The grim statistics range even higher when alcohol or drugs are involved.

• Access to a car provides additional opportunities for undesirable activities among teens, from drinking to premarital sex to visiting areas previously considered off-limits.

• Running a car is expensive enough without adding the cost of another driver to the overhead.

• It was hard keeping track of a teenage son's whereabouts when he was limited to foot or bike transportation. But now, with the access to wheels, the whole country can become his territory. When he earns a driver's license, Teen moves into a new area of freedom, and parents seem to lose what little control they had left.

Of course, there is a brighter side to this bleak picture. Teen drivers can and do relieve parents of annoying and disruptive chauffeuring chores. For the first month or two, they will *beg* to pick up the milk or get Little Brother at his Cub Scout meeting. Budding mechanics can often take over some of the car's maintenance requirements. And because the desire to drive is so intense, access to the car can become and remain a powerful bargaining tool. One bank officer recalls the college student who told her pointedly that he intended to default on his college loans. She told him that if he did so, his wages would be garnished, his income tax refund withheld, even his request for state licensing in his chosen field denied. He shrugged. But when she also mentioned that his driver's license would be suspended, the young man turned pale—and since graduation, has not missed a payment!

Before a driver's license becomes a reality, parents and Sixteen must sit down together and hammer out a set of guidelines that can make everyone feel comfortable. Actually, parents *never* feel comfortable when their offspring are out in cars, but these guidelines apply to behavior, not feelings.

Here are some ideas you may want to consider before having that talk with Sixteen and drawing up your own rules:

1. Who will teach your child to drive? The best way to assure

exposure to correct driving habits and attitudes is to have Sixteen enroll in his high school's driver's education program. It's a class just like Spanish or Chemistry, conducted regularly over a quarter or even a semester, where kids experience classwork, simulation machines and several hours out on the road with a teacher. If a school-sponsored driver's ed course is not available in your area, it's worth the money to send Sixteen to a commercial driving school. While parents or other adults are probably capable of teaching a youngster to drive, we often miss emphasizing the finer points or allow irritation (even fear) to get in the way. Professional instructors are used to the whole thing, know precisely what student must learn, and seem to have nerves of steel.

One caution—if your child turns sixteen while still a sophomore, he is legally entitled to earn a license. But usually it's not a good idea. Driving requires not only physical and mental skill but also a level of emotional maturity that most sophomores haven't yet attained.

2. Who will pay for the increased auto insurance premium, gasoline and other car costs that result when Teen becomes a licensed driver? It cannot be stressed too strongly that driving is a privilege, not a right. Youngsters have a right to food, clothing, shelter, medical care and other tangibles supplied by parents. However, they do not have a right to drive the family car. This *privilege* is granted to them under controlled conditions in exchange for responsible behavior. And one of the ways they demonstrate this responsible behavior is by paying for their share of the car's expenses. This experience prepares them for the reality of car ownership in the future, and also gives them a reason to handle the family car properly now. After all, if the insurance premium rises because of Teen's traffic tickets, or the gauge is on "E" because he forgot to gas up and now he's got an important date—who suffers? Teen, of course.

When your junior receives his learning permit, notify your auto insurance agent and ask him what the increase in your premium will be once Teen is added to the policy. Some companies give good driver discounts or lower rates if your student earns high grades in all his courses. Once you have the figure in dollars and cents, pick yourself up off the floor, present it to Sixteen, and work out a payment plan whereby he repays his share of the cost. Some kids prefer to pay their insurance on a monthly basis; others opt for an annual lump sum, usually due during the summer, when they are earning more money. As additional siblings are added to the family policy the premium will change, and it can be divided among them. This system keeps Mom and Dad's costs the same as they would be without any teenage drivers.

As to other expenses, many parents expect Sixteen to keep track of his mileage and supply that amount of gas. (When Teen is doing an errand for you, however, it's *your* gas.) Others ask him to simply put five or ten dollars into the tank each week, reasoning that it all evens out eventually. Maintenance can be a tricky issue. Most kids don't really have enough cash to contribute to a set of new tires or a tuneup, yet these are legitimate expenses that will go up now that another driver is wearing down the vehicle. An equitable trade-off might be to make Sixteen responsible for *overseeing* certain maintenance requirements, like putting air in tires, checking fluids and filters, taking the car in regularly for oil changes, while parents foot the bill. This plan teaches your adolescent about car costs and owner responsibility without draining his bank account.

So far we have been talking about a teenager driving the family car. But what happens when he starts pushing you for a car of his own?

Under normal circumstances, the minimum age for car ownership should be eighteen. Even though your junior has demonstrated personal and financial responsibility, providing a car for his exclusive use can open many doors which ought to stay shut a while longer. When a teenager owns his own car he can get preoccupied with it, to the detriment of school and other important priorities. Parental control over driving will diminish; the increased freedom may be too much for Teen to handle. The financial burden of sole ownership can be tremendous, too, siphoning earnings away from other things Teen may want or even need. No teen should own a car, of course, unless he buys and maintains it out of his own earnings.

Some households may have valid reasons for suspending these rules. If Mom doesn't drive, for instance, a teen with his own car can be a real help to her. Sometimes a special job opportunity presents itself, which may be worth the increased risk of car ownership for transportation. Occasionally a teen graduates early and needs a car for work or college. In these cases, guidelines will be different, but they should always be discussed prior to approving the purchase of a teenager's own car.

3. What sort of conduct should be expected from Sixteen when she is driving the family car? As we've mentioned, responsibilities go hand in hand with privileges. And unless Sixteen is willing to abide by the rules to which you and she have agreed, she obviously forfeits her privilege to use the family auto. Proper conduct should certainly include obeying traffic laws, refraining from drinking while driving, and returning home on time. You may also want to limit the number of passengers your young driver can take along, or restrict her from going certain places or from traveling too far from home. These restrictions can be eased as your child proves herself and gains more road experience.

Some parents find it helpful to draw up an official driving contract (see Chapter 8); Teen indicates that he will accept his responsibilities by signing the contract; if there are lapses, parents know that he is "reconsidering his driving privilege." This way, the decision to drive responsibly (or not to drive at all) is in Teen's lap.

Presenting a youngster with his first set of car keys is a moment we all face with trepidation and much soulsearching. But being a parent means "letting go," stage by stage, and this is yet another step in your child's road to maturity.

DROPPING OUT OF SCHOOL

Once in awhile, a child who is earning his own spending money, finally able to drive and has passed the age of sixteen which, in most states, signals an end to mandated education, decides to drop out of high school before he has graduated. This can be a time of great turmoil and even grieving for parents, who feel that they have failed to instill a love of learning in their child, and that he is doomed to a lifetime of second-class citizenship.

While this attitude is certainly understandable, dropping out is not necessarily the end of the world. Kids who do turn their

backs on classroom education have usually been having difficulty with academics for a long time, and often find other aspects of high school very unrewarding. They are anxious to "get
on with life," and often, the gap between what they can do—and
what educators and other adults expect them to do—has seemingly widened to a point of no return. If your adolescent is experiencing one academic failure after another, and is considering
leaving school, one stopgap measure may be a tutor, someone
who can help him close this chasm and raise his battered self-
image at the same time.

If you have already tried tutoring, or if your child rejects
such a solution, you may simply have to recognize that there is
no other choice—at least for now. The key is to leave the door
open for Teen to return to school later, once he has discovered
for himself that life is limited without a high school diploma.
This breakthrough, however, will come more readily if parents
avoid lecturing, "we told you so's" and other nagging. Parents
should also insist that Teen accept the consequences of his decision, that is, that he be financially self-sufficient (this would include Teen covering almost all of his personal bills, as well as
paying some room and board). The alternative is to shield Teen
from the realities of life by continuing to support him, and make
life easy for him, thus providing no motivation for him to re-
sume his studies.

In some cases, however, a high school dropout, finally freed
of the constraints of structured education, follows his own star
and becomes a marvelously-successful entrepreneur, an enter-
tainer or other success symbol—and ten or twenty years later,
decides to finish his classroom curriculum. This is not the easiest
route, and one few parents would choose, but it can and does
happen.

DATING

By the time your adolescent is sixteen, dating will also be on her
mind. Chances are, she's probably had a close circle of friends
since junior high, both boys and girls, and group activities have
been prevalent. And they will probably continue. One of the
nicer aspects of today's teen scene in many communities is that

kids are no longer pressured to pair up early. Instead it's not uncommon for an uneven group (say, two boys and four girls) to go to a movie together or arrange an informal party. It's also okay for girls to take the lead now and then, and even to drive, if they have custody of the family wheels tonight. A generation ago, members of the opposite sex were categorized quickly, as either a "love interest" or no relationship at all. But today's teens can have friends of both sexes without the need to get too quickly involved. And one helpful rule of thumb is to refuse to discuss specifics about dating until the situation actually materializes. Kathy may *talk* a lot about going out with boys, but until she's actually *asked* (or asks someone on her own), you really don't have to get too deeply involved in the philosophical whereases and what-if's.

When your teen does begin going out in a more formally-paired way, risks can be diminished by group dating—two or three couples attending a football game, then going to a pizzeria, for example. This arrangement is a good way for Teen to get to know someone without the stresses of one-on-one evenings. Eventually, of course, your adolescent will want to start single dating, and this urge is perfectly natural. Only by coming into contact with many boys during the coming years will she develop standards she needs to choose her permanent mate.

Dating brings up problems for parents, of course. When Daddy's little girl emerges from the bathroom looking like a mature woman and wafts out the door on the arm of a boy who Dad considers a carry-over from the caveman era, parents are apt to share a nervous night. When Son (who hasn't yet begun to shave) suddenly turns into a sophisticated man-about-town, fending off repeated phone calls from breathy females, Mom and Dad start to worry. It's natural to feel this way, especially in regard to one's children's sexual activity. We may trust our children, but we're not too sure we can trust their hormones. With one out of every ten teenage girls becoming pregnant each year, the concern is certainly justified.

SEXUAL ACTIVITY

Years ago, teenagers clearly knew what they could and could not do with their bodies. Today this is not the case. Our kids are bombarded with sexual stimulation through movies, ads, TV shows, magazines and rock music. Worse, the culture tells them that chastity is outdated: "If it feels good, it's fine!" Clinics dispense free birth control devices, classroom films presented by Planned Parenthood and other organizations promote the idea that "everybody's doing it." Even church leaders sometimes waffle, saying, "Well, it's really up to your own conscience . . . " In a culture that seems to condone teenage sexual activity, no wonder school counselors are seeing an increase in boys who break down and weep in their offices, wondering if something is wrong with them because they're still virgins. It's not surprising that a rising number of young girls are calling teen hotlines with the same question: "Is it all right to say no?"

Obviously our kids need a firm standard to live up to and protection from situations they cannot yet handle. Just as obviously, they are not going to get what they need from the media, from many professional organizations or from each other. Here, as in other troublesome areas, the family value system is of prime importance.

Ideally, you have been talking quite naturally with your children about sexuality from the time they lisped their first questions about it. But dispensing information is not enough, especially for teenagers. They need to fit this information into a behavioral structure, and they also need to know why such behavior is right or wrong. Therefore, it's important for parents to examine our own beliefs before attempting to pass them on to the kids. If we are not too sure of our own attitudes on sex, it will be very difficult to talk to teens about bodies and feelings. And when developing guidelines, it's important to base them on both moral values and common sense, rather than fear. Teen behavior that is motivated by fear, threats or power struggles is not nearly as effective or long-lasting as behavior stemming from knowledge and self-respect. Our first aim, perhaps, is to let our teens know that we believe in abstinence for unmarried teenagers. Far from being old-fashioned or an impossibility for today's kids, abstinence makes a lot of sense. Not only is it morally comfortable, but by living this way, a teen avoids much pressure. Our young people may bring up arguments for premarital sex, but often they are only bouncing such thoughts off of us to get our reactions. If we think otherwise, we will have to present facts to support our beliefs, such as the following:

1. Sexual intercourse can lead to pregnancy. Most teens are not ready for the job of parenting, which may mean forfeiting further education or premature entry into the work force.

2. Pregnancy can lead to abortion, which often leaves deep emotional scars. It is a sign of eliminating a problem rather than accepting the responsibility of one's actions.

3. Intercourse can lead to venereal diseases, which are now rampant and which can seriously affect one's future health.

4. Once a relationship includes intercourse, it's easy to begin another and another. Such activity leads to emotional and psychological confusion, the feeling of being used, a loss of dignity and self-respect. "There is a group of boys in my neighborhood who 'discovered' me last year," wrote a teenage girl in a poignant letter to a teen counseling service, outlining the promiscuous behavior she had begun in an attempt to assuage her loneliness. "I never thought anyone would want me, and it felt great ... for awhile. But now I hate myself for what I am doing, and sometimes I think about killing myself."

5. Premarital intercourse can make adultery easier after marriage. One can rightly ask, "If someone you love doesn't have the self-control to stay chaste *before* marriage, what about afterwards, when business trips, illnesses or other separations occur? Will you ever be completely confident?"

6. Finally, on a more personal level, "Why hurt yourself?" we can ask our teen. "You're special. And why hurt someone else who is just as special as you are?"

Teens should also understand that boys and girls are emotionally different. Part of nature's way of making sure that the human race continues is to ensure passionate and loving feelings between members of the opposite sex. The feelings themselves are natural and good; the sex drive is nothing to be ashamed of. But such feelings must be controlled. Since boys and girls do react differently to this drive, they should understand what their partner is experiencing.

When a girl is young and sexually inexperienced, she seldom feels any overpowering need for intercourse. Young girls who are promiscuous are usually acting out feelings of rebellion or anger, or searching for love rather than a physical release. Instead, a girl wishes to be kissed, caressed, and loved in a tender, non-genital way. She equates passion (of which she is certainly capable) and deep tenderness with love, and she assumes a boy feels the same way.

But a boy can make love without loving. Nature makes it remarkably easy for a teenage male to become sexually aroused. Although a boy knows that intercourse can result in serious consequences, and although he may care very deeply about his girl, it becomes increasingly difficult for him to hang onto his principles as he becomes sexually stimulated. Conscience all but vanishes in a fully aroused teenage male.

Given this difference in response, girls should be told not to tease boys sexually, by wearing provocative clothing designed to arouse them, by conducting sexually explicit conversations, or by allowing kissing and gentle touching to get out of control. A boy should be cautioned against putting the responsibility of control on the girl, against pretending that he loves her in order to gain sexual rewards, or against accusing her of being abnormal or frigid if she doesn't give in.

What about "safe sex?" In some school districts (and a lot more homes) handing a teenage boy a condom passes for "responsible sex education," the idea being that since it's impossible to expect teens to remain chaste, we their elders must at least protect them from any ill effects of their behavior. This logic fails on three points: first, condoms do not necessarily guarantee safe sex, that is, intercourse in which no disease will be passed, and no pregnancy will result. Public impressions to the contrary, recent studies are finding that the condom has about a 14% failure rate involving pregnancies, and an even higher rate of failure in disease (primarily AIDS) control.

Second, being informed about birth control doesn't necessarily mean that kids will use it when and if the moment arrives. Many teen mothers confirm that they knew all about pregnancy prevention, but didn't take it to heart. That's because a) teens typically live by the "it's not going to happen to me" attitude so prevalent in young people, and b) planning beforehand doesn't appeal to girls. It seems to indicate that they are promiscuous, and they don't like to think of themselves in that way (many would rather risk disease than their reputations). They prefer to believe that they were simply swept away in a moment of passion and couldn't help themselves. Often, this is quite true. In addition, many girls look upon pregnancy as an *improvement* over the home or school pressures being endured right now, and may be actually pleased to have a little "someone" all their own to love.

Third, we insult our kids when we treat them as little more than animals who are not capable of reaching for a higher level of behavior. Many kids, when presented with an alternative to "safe sex," are secretly relieved. In recent years, "abstinence rallies," drawing thousands of teenaged participants, have been held in many Midwest and southern cities; they are routinely ignored by the major news media, but apparently fill a special need for kids. Sex Respect, a federally-funded pilot program currently being taught in many Midwest junior highs and high schools, proves the point: based on a holistic health approach, rather than morality, it teaches students *why* to say "no" and *how* to say "no." Pilot schools have noticed a definite drop in teen pregnancies, as well as an increasing number of students interested in taking the class. (Follow-up statistics record a significant change in attitude among students exposed to the "everybody's *not* doing it, and you don't have to either" approach.) One of the most popular parts of Sex Respect is the chapter on secondary virginity. "Don't buy the myth that once you've 'lost it,' you can no longer control your sexual impulses," the text advises. "After all, if you gain ten pounds over Christmas break, it doesn't mean you have to gain ten pounds on spring break. If you take money from someone's locker, it doesn't mean you have to keep on stealing." Other wholesome programs are springing up around the country too, and we do our children a real disservice if we assume they won't be receptive to this type of message.

In addition to talking frankly about these issues, and reassuring teens that their feelings are normal but that they *can* control them, parents have an obligation to protect kids from situations that may be too hot to handle. This can take many forms:

• **Make sure parties are chaperoned and no liquor is available,** since alcohol lowers the threshold of control.

• **Encourage teens to date a variety of partners,** rather than team up with a steady. Many singles become a duo simply because it's easier than being alone; some date for status, too. Help your daughter determine her motives. Does she really care for this boy or is she clinging to him for security? What would happen if she went dateless for a while? Or went out with someone else? If a couple does seem attracted to each other exclusively, don't force them apart. Direct intervention will only drive them more determinedly into each other's arms. You can, however, set limits on the amount of time they can spend in each other's company.

• **Don't leave an empty house accessible to teens.** Be in the background at group activities. Make sure dating couples use your car for transportation only, rather than simply for riding around.

• **Don't send mixed messages.** Discussing birth control methods is fine in the context of general information. But the parent who sends her coed daughter off to college with a prescription for the pill, "just in case," is certainly condoning sexual activity, despite what she may preach to the contrary.

• **Be available to your teens;** talk about any subject they bring up. Don't act shocked, and don't presume that they will act on information you provide. And if you're a bit embarrassed, admit it. "We didn't talk this frankly when I was a teen, and sometimes I don't know how to explain something to you. But I love you, and you need the facts, so I'll keep trying." Such an attitude speaks volumes. Sometimes, despite the love, care and instruction that good parents provide, teens get sexually involved anyway. If you know your adolescent is "sleeping around" or is intimately involved with one person, seek out a family counselor who shares your views and can deal with the underlying causes for your teen's behavior. Many sexually active teens are not simply acting on their powerful physical drives; sometimes they're trying to prove their own worth, looking for love and acceptance, or rebelling. These motives must be dealt with before graver matters develop.

PREMARITAL PREGNANCY

Almost a million unmarried teenage girls become pregnant each year in America. The result is a tragic situation not only for the girl, who is usually ill equipped for the responsibilities of pregnancy and parenting, but also for the young father and for both sets of parents as well. In some cases boys bolt, refusing to admit paternity or to shoulder responsibilities. Parents react with shock, guilt, tears, anger, emotional scenes. At a time when she most needs the support of others, a young girl is sometimes left to deal with this problem on her own. How does she handle it?

A small percentage of out-of-wedlock teen pregnancies result in marriage to the baby's father. While this solution makes sense for older couples already engaged or planning marriage in the future, it's a poor option for younger teens. The high failure rate among marrying teens, whether pregnant or not, proves conclusively that most are not mature enough for the commitment that marriage demands. An impending birth puts an even greater strain on this shaky union.

Almost half of pregnant teenagers abort their babies. Often they are pressured into this act by well-meaning parents or clinic counselors who regard abortion as the easiest and least painful solution. Recent research, however, indicates that the emotional scars left by deliberately destroying one's unborn child can be greater than the trauma of carrying that child to term. Abortion can also cause sterility, disease, a damaged uterus and other complications which can affect later childbearing—even at the sterility rate of one percent (which is generally accepted among experts), this means that forty women each day (one percent of 4000 daily abortions) are aborting the last child they will ever conceive. Many of these women may be teenagers, unaware of the heartbreaking situation they may be creating for themselves and future spouses. Pregnancy steals perhaps a year from a young woman's life, but the psychological and physical aftermath of abortion can hurt her for a long time.

Almost half of today's pregnant teenagers elect to have their babies and raise them. If a strong and supportive family unit is available, this can sometimes work. But often the immature mother is thrown out on her own with few resources, limited job skills and schooling, little or no money (a young man can be legally required to help support a child he fathered, but usually his financial resources are extremely limited). More than 40% of teenage girls who drop out of high school cite pregnancy as the reason; half of high school mothers are living in poverty by their mid-twenties, many with more than one child. Pressures grow heavier, robbing a young woman of emotional balance, sometimes causing her to resent or abuse her baby. Sadly, her child is cheated out of a stable home environment and often grows up to repeat the cycle.

About 4% of pregnant teens decide to have their babies and place them up for adoption. Although giving up an infant can be traumatic, this solution seems to create the least amount of permanent damage to the mother. A pregnant teen, whether she plans to keep her infant or give it up, can continue her education, live at home or in a temporary care facility, and receive counselling before and after delivery. She can return to her interrupted life unencumbered with a marriage or infant she wasn't yet ready to handle. She will grieve deeply, and she will miss her baby for years to come, perhaps forever. But she will have brought something positive out of a negative ordeal, and her feelings of self-respect may help her build a better tomorrow.

Clearly, none of these solutions is a happy one. But if your daughter is pregnant, try to give her the help and support that she desperately needs. Birthright and Catholic Charities are two national organizations that offer counselling not only for pregnant girls but for their families, too.

And do not overlook a boy's reaction. Many young men are not as callous about pregnancy as they are portrayed to be. They are deeply affected by the idea of becoming a parent, and can benefit by counseling. Such services are now available to a boy's parents too; these potential grandparents, while not receiving the same degree of attention as the parents of the pregnant girl, may be deeply hurt at the prospect of losing a grandchild; in any case, they will have to support their son through this situation. Ideally, such counselling should include both young parents as well as *their* parents and their siblings. Everyone involved needs to take some time to sort through their feelings, and resolve the situation as well as they can.

AIDS AND VENEREAL DISEASE

In addition to pregnancy, sexually active teenagers also run the risk of contracting a venereal disease. Because these diseases are transmitted through intercourse, those who contract them are often reluctant to seek treatment and to confide names of sexual partners who may have passed on the disease. In this way the incidence of VD continues to increase, now second in number only to the common cold as a national ailment.

Although more resistant strains of VD are developing, various antibiotics still cure syphilis, gonorrhea and lesser known types of VD in the early stages. Without treatment, VD can cause blindness, paralysis, heart disease or sterility. At the moment, the most common sexually transmitted disease is chlamydia—more than four million cases each year. Women often have no identifiable symptoms, yet without antibiotic treatment, the disease can damage fallopian tubes, and cause eventual infertility.

Genital herpes, however, can stay with a person for life despite treatment, infecting partners whenever the disease is active. Thirty million Americans currently suffer from herpes, and the epidemic is spreading at the rate of 500,000 new cases every year. Not only is the disease painful and frustrating, women with herpes run the risk of cervical cancer as well as infecting future unborn babies.

Teens must be informed about VD—how it is contracted, what symptoms it causes. They especially need to be told that VD can be avoided completely by remaining chaste until marriage. While it is to be hoped that teens would inform their parents at the first sign of VD, such an expectation is unrealistic. Instead, most kids usually appear for treatment at a confidential teen clinic, probably the same clinic that dispenses birth control devices and even performs abortions, all without parental knowledge or consent. But VD services these clinics provide are helpful to those teens who wouldn't dream of letting Mom or Dad know. If your teen does happen to describe symptoms such as genital discharge or sores, painful urination, swollen glands, rash, loss of hair—and, in the case of herpes, flu-like symptoms which lead to genital blisters—get him or her to your family doctor right away.

Another consequence of premarital intercourse is AIDS (Acquired Immune Deficiency Syndrome), a fatal medical condition caused by infection with the AIDS virus, which breaks down the body's normal immune system. Teens can get infected with AIDS in three major ways: from having sex with an infected person, from sharing hypodermic needles with an infected person or through a transfusion with infected blood (although these odds have been significantly lowered due to better testing of blood donors). Initial symptoms include swollen lymph nodes, weight loss, diarrhea, fever or sweats and deep persistent fatigue.

"When my friends talk about AIDS, it's usually a joke," one teen sums up the reaction of this age group to the possibility of contracting a disease which continues to be primarily connected to homosexual behavior. But more than 20% of people with AIDS are in their twenties, and many were infected as teenagers by heterosexual partners; the AIDS virus may not cause symptoms for as long as ten years. It has been estimated that AIDS will eventually be one of the top five killers of young people.

Since AIDS spreads primarily through multiple sexual partners—and is therefore one of the most easily preventable diseases in society today—it's further proof that nature is probably trying to tell us something, that abstinence before marriage and monogamy afterwards are norms which serve the survival needs of mankind. Explained this way, your sixteen-year-old may roll his eyes and sigh, but secretly, he'll admit to the logic of it all.

The vast majority of today's kids are not preoccupied with venereal disease or premarital pregnancy; their concerns are more elementary. They look forward to dating with both a wholesome enthusiasm and a hint of trepidation. How do I say no? Do I have to "make a move"? Will someone ask me to the dance? What if she drops me? Will anyone ever love me? You can't protect your child from all the pain and uncertainty of this time of life, nor can you provide every answer. But you can inform her, remain vigilant and be there to comfort and sustain her as she moves into this risky but exciting world.

TESTS

While your junior "gets it all together," dips his toes into the work world, earns a driver's license, and begins to date, new things are happening in school as well. If he had an extremely fulfilling sophomore year and didn't experience a slump in grades, he may have one now. Juniors, too, sometimes get sick of school. But many Sixteens take their class duties seriously, and begin to focus on subjects they enjoy: auto mechanics, home ec, science. They also anticipate career choice. Do I want to go on to college? A trade or technical school? Join the military? Get a full-time job?

Career planning will be discussed more fully in the next chapter, but parents—especially those rearing their first teenager—will be interested to know that many college placement tests are taken in the *junior* year, not the senior year, which would seem more logical. High schools notify their students of these tests early on and offer reams of preparatory material in the counselling office. But if your teenage offspring is typical, he either forgets to collect the stuff, or it winds up under his bed.

So, for your information:

• The PSAT (Preliminary Scholastic Aptitude Test)/NMSQT (National Merit Scholarship Qualifying Test) is a two-hour version of the SAT (Scholastic Aptitude Test), all of which measure verbal and math abilities. The PSAT/NMSQT is taken in October of the junior year, and is recommended for all juniors in the top half of their class scholastically. The PSAT is a practice test for the SAT, taken later in the year. Its score is not used for college admission. But if a student scores well, he may be named a National Merit finalist and be granted a partial college scholarship. There is a minimal fee for this test, usually payable at the time it is taken.

• The SAT is required for admission to many private colleges and universities. Students must register for this test by mailing the forms and fee six weeks prior to the test. SATs are conducted in May or June of the junior year, then offered again in the fall of the senior year. In many states, the results of the junior year

SAT are automatically forwarded to the state scholarship program.

• The ACT (American College Testing program) is a battery of admissions, scholarship, guidance, and placement tests, required for admission into many public schools. The ACT can be taken in April or June of the junior year, October or December of the senior year. The results of junior year testing are also sent to the state's scholarship program. Registration and fees are due six weeks before testing. Many kids take the SAT and ACT in the spring of their junior year in order to be considered for scholarships, as well as early application for college. They may retake the tests in senior year if they want to raise their scores for late college entrance. Colleges usually do not require both tests, so if your teen already has a firm college choice, and he meets the other requirements for admission, he need only take the test that school requires. If your family is not financially well off, you can apply through a school counselor for a waiver of test fees.

Even if your child is now uncertain about his college plans, it's a good idea for him to take the tests at the proper times. They are a requirement for entrance to college, and once completed, he will have one less thing to worry about when considering future plans. Your high school guidance and counselling department has forms, samples, practice tests and other information for you, including what universities require which tests. Contact them, and don't let the deadlines slip by.

Junior year—coming to grips with grades, jobs, social life, more and more adult responsibilities. Learning to look at the future. Soon, all too soon, that future will be here.

Chapter 5

Senior:
The Year of Decision

*An adolescent becomes an adult three years
before his parents think he does, and
about two years after he thinks he does.*
General Lewis B. Hershey, 1951

King and Queen of the hill, the Big Guys, the Number Ones. It's senior year, and your adolescent basks in his position.

He's changed a great deal in these past three years. Yesterday he sneaked into a classroom, hoping no one would notice. Today he swaggers in, hoping everyone will see him. He seems sure of himself, less intimidated than he used to be. Instead of wondering what he can do for you, he seems to be asking what you can do for him. In short, he's at the pinnacle of his high school career.

But it isn't over yet. There's a whole year ahead, with plenty of emotionally laden issues to confront. By the time a teenager reaches senior year, parents often regard him as an adult, assuming that he has attained the maturity and skill level necessary to handle his own life. But this really isn't true. Seniors have grown and changed enormously since they started high school, but only a handful are completely ready to assume an adult role. The majority still need parental guidance and support as they work through the issues that surface in this last year of high school.

What are these issues? And how can parents help?

FEAR OF THE FUTURE

Teenagers are paradoxical, caught between conflicting desires. They begin to snip the bonds of parental attachment, which is a wholesome phase of growth, but then they start to experience disquieting and fearful feelings: What's out there? What am I running *to*? Can I cope? At times they long to revert to childhood, to be protected, sheltered, held and cared for again. But they also feel driven to surge ahead, to attain the adult status just beyond their grasp. This unsettled situation creates anxiety, and teens cope with anxiety in a variety of ways—covering it with arrogance, bullying or bragging, running from it by using drugs or alcohol. Psychologists have long known that the more self-esteem a teen possesses, the less anxiety he suffers. But in senior year, even the most self-confident boy or girl will face some uncertainty. Why?

Up until now, life has been pretty predictable. Grade school, high school, familiar friends and neighborhood and always Mom and Dad were there to see that Teen stayed within certain boundaries, there to take over on a decision that he couldn't or wouldn't attempt, there to pick up the pieces. Now, however, the senior recognizes that this security is soon going to be removed. He will no longer be sheltered and protected; instead, he is expected to make his own decisions and accept responsibility for his life. In one respect, it's a healthy, long-awaited moment. But to the paradoxical teen, such impending freedom can also provide fear and even depression. How do seniors cope with this fear of the future?

Some simply delay facing it. In a variety of subtle ways, they hold onto dependence just a little longer. A boy who has been doing fairly well in high school suddenly fails several courses in senior year, guaranteeing that he will not graduate on time. A girl who was looking forward to going away to college begins to shift gears, deciding that the local junior college seems a better solution. Junior colleges can be excellent choices for many reasons, but sometimes they allow Teen to postpone growing up.

Others act out their fears by a heightened interest in wild behavior, most notably beer parties. One California high school survey found that 72% of its seniors had used alcohol within the last thirty days. While some of this activity can be attributed to the ongoing problem of youthful alcoholism, it also signals the rising anxiety level among most high school seniors.

Seniors continue to test limits, sometimes quarreling with parents over dating, driving and curfews—issues that seemed settled last year. "Hey, I'm grown up now!" they seem to say. "You can't keep me a baby any longer!" And yet in their juvenile tantrums, and disregard for authority, they are anything *but* adults.

Some fourth-year students begin to slow down, too—daydreaming, slipping into apathy in the classroom or at home, going through the motions but not really staying "with it." Often this lethargy is a cover-up for inner turmoil and confusion: Am I going to be able to take care of things, to make the right choices? Like Scarlett O'Hara, they'll think about it tomorrow.

LOSS

Any change involves laying aside the old and putting on the new. Soon the new becomes familiar and comfortable too, and is once again exchanged. Such is the rhythm of growth.

But in laying aside the familiar, we often experience a sense of loss. This person, this item, this habit has been a part of us, and we relinquish it reluctantly. Nowhere is this sense of loss more profound than in senior year when a teen says goodbye to his routine, his school, his teachers, his friends. Even if he will continue to live at home, he knows that things will never again be the same. Exciting adventures loom on the horizon, but he is not experiencing them yet. For now he is severing the relationships that have meant so much to him. The old gang, the peer group which sustained and buffered him throughout the past several years, will splinter now, never to be reclaimed or experienced in quite the same way.

This situation can become even more acute when a close boy-girl relationship is involved. The couple has grown emotionally dependent on each other, spends a lot of time in one another's company, has developed deep feelings of love and trust for one another. In many ways, they have provided each other's security. Now the security is threatened, and the couple must deal with questions such as: Should I go to college if you're not going? Should we go to the same school? Should we get married? Should we stay single for now, but become sexually intimate? One of the most basic forms of security is physical closeness; teens who are going through periods of stress or anxiety are especially vulnerable to the temptation and temporary release of love-making.

CAREER PLANS

Today's high school senior cannot afford to wait until graduation to make choices which will affect his future. Even though, at seventeen, he may have little or no idea of what he wants to do or where he wants to go, it matters not. He must select a path and make plans anyway.

But this generation of teenagers seems to be short on idealism. They are disillusioned by what they perceive as a society filled with opportunists and fakes, Watergates, corporate sleaze, the bomb, economic uncertainty. They aren't sure they can change the world (aren't sure they even want to try). But this skepticism helps them make more sober and realistic assessments of their future. "Young people are willing to work hard and to get ahead," says one priest and observer of today's youth, "but without the enthusiasm of the past, they have a critical view of the way things are run and are skeptical of those in authority. Yet they feel they have no choice. This is the only world at their disposal." The current generation differs from the 1950s teen who, while also wanting to become part of the mainstream, rarely questioned or criticized the status quo. Our kids are also at variance with the teen of the 1960s generation, who operated primarily on idealism, often carried to an extreme. Because of their lack of enthusiasm, many of today's seniors find it especially hard to pin down a career choice and follow through on it. They're not at all sure that their effort will make a difference—in their own lives or in the lives of others. This crowd of graduates is also more worried about financial security than the generations just passed; when interviewed, many already doubt they'll be able to afford the kind of economic lifestyle their parents attained.

Still, a bewildering array of options lie open to today's senior, and given his lack of perspective about these options, his choices become even tougher. Pressured into deciding among college or junior college, the military, or the job market, our seniors get the feeling that whatever they choose is "written in stone": if this alternative doesn't work, they've ruined their entire lives. A highschooler doesn't have the benefit of hindsight, experience or wisdom gained through years of adult living. From his view, each decision is monumental, its implications unbearable. He isn't *sure*—what if he makes a *mistake*?

THE ROLE OF THE PARENTS

One of our most important tasks during this period is to communicate, and to keep avenues open so that Senior can communicate too. If your teen is grappling with some perplexing decisions yet he won't open up to you, how will you know what he needs and what you can do to help? If yours is a home where kids are free to speak out, however, try breaking the ice with a few comments like the following:

"You're going to miss your pals, aren't you?"

"Are you finding it hard to make a decision about college?"

"There are so many things to think about in senior year, aren't there?"

When your son does respond, reassure him that his confused feelings are perfectly normal. Loss *is* a difficult issue to deal with, but he has handled it before and he can cope again. Making choices is scary, and a teen especially needs to know that while these decisions are important ones, none—with the exception of marriage—involves a lifetime commitment. It's natural to be ambivalent about college vs. career, which college, what job. But many people (including those much more experienced than Teen) start out along one road, then discover that a detour seems more appropriate. And this is *okay*. The future holds no guarantees; all that is expected of Teen is to handle today, to make the choices that seem best, and to get on with it. Time will tell whether the correct decision has been made. If not, another will be available.

This philosophy can often reassure the anxious senior. She needs to know that it is permissible to be uncertain, that it is all right to come to a conclusion or two without being able to see the next fifty years clearly in focus. Parents can also help teens to make wise decisions by talking over the issues involved.

CHOOSING MARRIAGE

Most parents, no matter how much they may like their youngster's "steady," are not eager to encourage a teen marriage; we know only too well the grim failure rate of such unions. It's not enough to say "no," however, especially when our teens are legal adults and can wed without our consent. Asking pertinent questions may encourage the kids to wait awhile.

What questions to ask:

1. Are you both emotionally mature, able to defer gratification, put the other's needs ahead of your own and accept responsibility in a sensible manner? Are you still having an "identity crisis," wondering who you are and how you want to live, asking questions that ought to be answered before you choose a job or marriage?

Emotional immaturity is probably the primary cause of marriage failure. Young people sometimes marry in order to solve an ego crisis, to avoid the hard work of growing up, to leave a difficult home life or to gain security. What is your real reason for marrying?

2. Have you had enough experience for marriage? Discovering life, developing values and patterns, growing emotionally and intellectually are all jobs that a young person must do, at best before he links his life with another. Will a marriage make such necessary growth easier for you, or will you be stunted and narrowed instead?

3. Have you a wise financial plan? Have you researched the cost of housing, utilities, food, insurance, furniture, clothing, transportation and other necessities—can your income handle it? Will you have extra cash for fun, for illness, for a baby? Or will every dime be needed just for sustenance? If so, what kind of life will this be? (If there is a Marriage and Family class available in your child's high school, encourage her to take it, preferably in senior year; students must address many of these issues in practical terms, and many have their starry eyes opened!)

4. Is there a cultural or religious gap between the two of you? If marriage partners come from noticeably different backgrounds, problems are inevitable. Does he disapprove of working wives? Does she have many interests that he cannot share? In what faith will the children be raised? If these differences are marked, is it possible that the physical attraction is so strong that it has blotted out all other considerations? Is physical attraction alone the firmest foundation for a lifetime commitment?

5. Finally, can you consider waiting a while? If you *can't*, is it because you are afraid the relationship cannot stand the test of time or distance? Are you riding the crest of an emotional wave rather than thinking clearly about your future?

Sometimes these questions, discussed sympathetically rather than angrily, can clear the air and defer marriage plans. But if you and your teen have discussed all of the issues above, and he or she is still adamant about marrying, then you can do little else but stand by and provide love and understanding. The kids are going to need it.

Becoming In-laws—"Mom, we're getting married!" is a phrase that usually brings happiness and a feeling of "rightness" about it—but not, unfortunately, when the bride and groom are teenagers. As parents of a couple barely old enough to drive, much less marry, you will no doubt find it harder to adopt a "hands-off" policy than parents of couples marrying at a later age. Knowing how far to go when offering advice, help or financial support is tricky in the most ideal situations, so you are to be forgiven for the confusion you'll undoubtedly suffer about these issues. Your bewilderment will be even more pronounced if a pregnancy is also involved: just how are the children going to support a child without our help?

Experts agree that extended families help hold marriages together; a warm and loving in-law relationship provides an extra measure of support and affirmation for the young couple as they work out their own patterns of living together. But "supporting" is not the same as "controlling," and for parents of very-young marrieds, the line can get somewhat blurred. A few tips may help couples remember the difference:

• Begin as you mean to go on. Remember that it's the couple's wedding, and let them decide what they'd like (as long as it is financially feasible). Even if the bride wants her attendants to

wear black or prefers the ceremony held in someone's base-
ment, refuse to interfere. This will set a wholesome precedent as
other matters arise.

• Refuse to take sides as the inevitable disagreements begin.
Treat the couple as a *couple*, resisting the impulse to take sides,
play the Blame Game (everything that goes wrong in the marriage must be *his/her* fault) or singling out your child for special
attention or confidences. If you're used to speaking your mind
and/or giving advice, go ahead, but don't ask Follow-up questions on the final outcome; newlyweds who feel free to make up
their own minds will be far more open to the opinions of their
elders.

• Offering financial help is always a dubious undertaking,
but in the case of extremely young couples, it may be appropriate. However, it's more tactful (and more helpful in the long
run) to put this aid in the form of practical help—asking them
over to dinner right before payday; finding a garage-sale "bar-
gain" that would look perfect in the living room; offering free
babysitting so the young couple can take a break from responsibilities—than to simply write checks. In addition, young couples
often overextend themselves with credit purchases, and paying
these bills off—however long the road to fiscal responsibility—is
going to teach them more than they would learn if you stepped
in.

When teenagers marry, parental authority and involvement
end with unaccustomed abruptness, and for awhile, you may
have trouble getting used to your role change. If you find yourself continuing to hang on and stay too closely involved in the
couple's daily lives, you may need to do some work on *yourself*
rather than the kids.

CHOOSING COLLEGE

A college education is not for everyone. Surely a boy or girl who
has been notably unenthusiastic about academics and has earned mediocre grades during school should not be pressured into
attending college (and with so many universities tightening admission standards, may not be accepted). There are other options open to this youngster, more in keeping with her talents

and interests.

College should also not be attempted if your offspring is opposed to it strongly, even if her grades are good. A college curriculum is usually very demanding. It takes real commitment and dedication on the student's part, especially if she must also hold a part-time job to make ends meet. A teen who is really reluctant about college, not just normally nervous, shouldn't be forced. A few years from now she may be eager for the chance, and will make better use of it.

If your son or daughter does want to go to college and has the required grade point average and test scores, your first consideration is going to be financial. Don't wait until senior year to decide how much money you can afford to spend on college! Even if you aren't sure of the exact amount you'll have available, it's much better to start saving early, and discussing financial matters with your college-bound student when she's a sophomore or junior. She'll need to plan her own savings program in light of the information you share, well before additional financial sources are explored. Financial limits will also have bearing on the colleges she considers. If you can't afford to send her to Harvard, let her know early in the game. There's nothing crueler than being accepted at one's dream school, only to discover that the money won't be there. However, despite the presumably horrifying statistics about college costs, you needn't be unduly alarmed—plenty of ordinary, middle-income families manage to send their kids to college, and you probably can too. College costs *have* increased dramatically in recent years. Tuition and fees average about $8700 annually at four-year private colleges; about $1700 annually at four-year public schools (double that if your child lives out-of-state) and about $850 at two-year public colleges. Room and board runs between $2500 and $3000 at most institutions but, as you can well imagine, doesn't cover the entire cost of food. Nor do these figures include books, clothes, transportation and recreation costs, which can vary widely depending on your child's standard of living. While the cost of a college education has increased, state and federal aid for students has been cut, and eligibility requirements tightened. Financial aid is supposed to go to the neediest students; in reality, those who know how to apply for it will probably receive more than those who don't. For example:

- Although your child will probably not be eligible for a PELL (federal government grant), she must apply for one before any other aid can even be considered.
- Formerly, families with adjusted gross incomes of $30,000 or less qualified automatically for Guaranteed Student Loans; now every family must prove need.
- A family's expected college contribution can actually be computed in three different ways, depending on the kind of school your child picks, and where you live; aid also depends on the size of your family, the age of the older parent, how many people attend college, the cost of the college itself . . . obviously, there's no real rule of thumb. Despite this supposedly-bleak picture, kids are attending college today in record numbers. How? A rare student receives outright grants or scholarships for a portion of her expenses, based either on need, high grades or a particular sport or activity subsidy such as band or debate. Others may receive guaranteed loans up to $2500 per year with no interest charged until after they graduate (these are also need-based). In families not eligible for direct low-interest student loans, parents can take PLUS loans up to $4000 per year in their name, paying only the interest until after graduation (when, presumably, the student will take over repayment of the principal). In some instances, corporations employing parents will offer similar loan opportunities.

Many kids are also employed under college work-study programs or find part-time jobs in the university town, similar to the work they did while living at home; a small percentage join the Reserve Officers Training Corps (ROTC), a campus army recruitment program which gives scholarships and other aid if students commit themselves to a three-year stint in the service. Through a combination of programs, the "impossible dream" can become real, especially for kids who are highly motivated and have planned well.

Planning begins with your youngster's high school counselling department. Make an appointment early in senior year, and get as much information as you can. In general, the steps are: 1) Acceptance at a college (admission to more than one may be granted before Teen makes the final decision); 2) Application for financial aid from the college by submitting proper forms; 3) Application for a loan (type will depend on your eligibility) through your bank or college; 4) Search for other scholarships for which your youngster may be eligible.

The high school counselor will guide you through these initial steps. It is, however, your teenager's responsibility to seek out and apply for any private scholarships that might be available. You can find possibilities by checking certain publications (see Chapter 9); many of these books are available for loan in the counselor's office. Remember that although you start this process in the fall of senior year, financial aid forms cannot be filed until after ACT/SAT tests have been taken and after January 1 of the year your child will start college, since you will be providing financial information from your current tax form. If your teenager is seeking early admission, these steps will have to be taken earlier after consultation with the high school counselor.

Junior College. Most large communities have a junior college in their midst, and this facility offers the perfect compromise between a four-year university and no college at all. As the name implies, junior college offers only a two-year program. Kids who are considering a bachelor's degree can take the required freshman and sophomore courses here, then transfer to a university for classes in their major field. Kids who are not interested in a four-year course of study and want training in a particular field can opt for a two-year associate degree in computer science, horticulture, hotel management, paralegal work and other practical fields.

Junior colleges are quite flexible; courses are available year-round, both day and evening. Because they're community-based, junior colleges often work with area employers to develop specific business courses. Students can sustain part- or full-time jobs with ease, and lower tuition costs are more manageable. Best of all, this option allows some hesitant high school graduates—and others less mature than their peers at this point in their lives—to continue their educations without yet making the break from home. The main financial drawback to junior college is that a car may be needed for transportation; be sure to add it as overhead when considering your college budget. Also, it is rare for junior college attendees to be granted federal aid; this usually happens only if several other family members are also attending college. The other drawback to junior college is that there are fewer opportunities to make friends. Unlike the close living arrangements in the dorms, sororities and fraternities at universities, a junior college student may feel like a number, unconnected with school except for his few weekly classes. But many kids don't miss this at all; their lives are busy enough and they have only one purpose at school—to learn. For them, junior college can be a good experience, a bridge between high school and the career world.

CHOOSING THE MILITARY

With the country's current emphasis on the all-volunteer army, as well as the continuing manpower needs of other branches of the service, signing up for a hitch makes sense for some of today's seniors. The Army, Navy, Air Force and Marines offer youngsters a chance to see the world, to enrich their perspectives on life, to gather experience, to earn a modest income and to be trained for a career, all at the same time. Depending on the program, kids in service also earn money for later college tuition. Military recruiters make themselves very available to high school juniors and seniors. They will give talks at school, send literature to interested students or phone them at home for lengthier chats. If your senior sees the military as a possibility, be sure to accompany him to school-sponsored talks or appointments at the recruiting office. Get *all* your questions answered before helping your senior make a decision.

CHOOSING THE WORK WORLD

Some seniors just don't want any more formal learning, at least not now. They're eager to join the Real World, where the action is. A fortunate few know exactly what they want to do, but most are apt to flounder a bit. What kind of a job should I look for? *And what if I don't like it?* A first step in the job search is defining talents and interests. Help your son or daughter "get it all together" by asking the following questions:

What kind of part-time and summer jobs have you held? What did you like about them? What did you dislike? Why? What personal qualities do you have that will make you good at certain kinds of work? Patience? Leadership? Ability to organize? Enjoyment of people?

What school courses did you like best? What extracurricular activities have you participated in? Why did you enjoy them? What are your volunteer activities? Your hobbies? Special talents?

What type of job interests you now? What would you like to be doing five years from now? What sort of job should you seek now in order to prepare for that goal?

Once your youngster has zeroed in on a particular career area (and this may take a while), his next step is to apply for a job, by filling out an application, by having a personal interview, or both. Before he undergoes either procedure, make sure he knows how to fill out an application; have him compile his work history and pertinent dates, the details of his formal education (including any honors), names and addresses of references, and his social security number. Assembling this material beforehand will make it easier for him to handle himself in the personnel department. You can also run through a mock interview with Teen, if he's amenable. Such interviews can be fun. Has he learned all he can about the company? His prospective position? Has he dressed conservatively? Does he answer questions frankly but briefly, and with interest? Does he slouch, mumble or chew gum? Does he criticize former employers, give excuses, or ramble?

"So many of today's kids are interested in two things," says the owner of a small business. "How much do I get paid, and how little do I have to work? Give me an alert, polite youngster who isn't afraid to do *more* than his share—and I'll find a spot for him."

Reassure your youngster that feelings of trepidation are normal, and also make sure she knows that an initial job choice does not bind her to the company until retirement. If she should eventually discover that she doesn't like her job, there's no disgrace in searching for another. What's important now is *beginning*, working conscientiously, and building credentials, skills and self-confidence.

When contemplating the job market, your senior may discover that although she doesn't want college, she does need some additional training before she can apply for the job she seeks. If so, you may want to investigate secretarial or business schools, trade or technical institutes, union apprenticeships and the like. Talk to your child's counselor and to friends and relatives in the line of work your offspring seeks; encourage her to talk with them, too, as sympathetic sources of information and advice, if not actual job leads. And thoroughly check out any institution that offers specialized training. Some have long-standing reputations which can be easily verified, while a handful may be nothing more than high-priced rip-offs.

A high school senior, poised on the edge of maturity, may *seem* as though she is an adult. Parents are often tempted to adopt a hands-off policy, abandoning our roles as teachers and protectors. "What can we teach her now?" we wonder. But our seniors are not all grown up, not yet. They still need the structure and order we provide, they still need, every now and then, to lean back on our rules in order to get themselves out of harmful situations. If the rules have been withdrawn too early, kids find themselves with too much freedom too soon. It's important for us not to throw in the towel, just because Janet is becoming so poised, so self-confident.

At the other end of the spectrum are the parents who are still overprotecting their young. While it's important for us to stand pat on behavior guidelines, we should also make sure that our senior is able to handle the practical requirements of life.

"A home should be structured," says a school psychologist, "but once in a while, there is too much structure. Mom is still making Seventeen's sandwiches, ironing his shirts, doing all the shopping . . . Dad hands the kids money when they need it, offering little or no training in budgeting or long-range planning." Part of a senior's uncertainty may stem from his incompetency in these areas, and incompetency often comes from not enough practice on his own.

In guiding your senior through his last year, therefore, be sure to teach him any practical skills that may have been overlooked earlier. He needn't be a culinary master, but he should surely know how to prepare simple meals *and* how to wash the dishes correctly. Does he know that red shirts are not to be laundered with white ones, that bleach isn't poured directly on fabric? Can she shop intelligently for groceries or clothes, make up a budget and stick to it? If she does not already have a checking account, will she soon learn to handle one?

"Senior year can be an emotional one not only for kids, but also for their parents," says this psychologist. "There's a tendency to wonder if we did a good job raising the kids. We look back, realizing the things we *should* have done but didn't, the lost opportunities. We get depressed; or worse, we suddenly set tight limits in order to make up for all the things we didn't do."

The solution for your child, he believes, is to look at the *general* behavior of your boy or girl, rather than the specifics. Does this senior handle school well? Is he on time for team practice, reliable at work? Despite occasional moodiness, is he usually decent to those around him, competent at basic tasks? Although he may often disagree with parents or other authority figures, does he usually respect them? If so, your senior is *fine*, despite his all-too-frequent lapses.

But if you spot a few troublesome areas, you might want to approach the situation by saying, "I really feel you're doing a competent job, but I'm worried about a couple of things. Can we talk?"

If, however, your senior seems to be in constant conflict with authority, has failing grades, poor job performance and an apparent lack of inner controls, then family counselling is certainly indicated. A senior is not yet an adult, but he should be displaying adult behavior at least part of the time. If he can't or won't, he may need extra time to learn the personal skills he has missed. And this catch-up time will be far more valuable under the care of a counselor.

In this looking-back process, parents also need to realize that part of our discomfort stems from the letting-go process we must all endure. Any kind of major life-change involves some grieving (whether it is recognized or not) and some upset; it's as if you've been stirring a pail of water in one direction for a long time, and the flow has not been interrupted. Now you are changing directions and for a time, until the new stream becomes smooth, there will be choppy waters. You may find yourself getting inexplicably involved in powere struggles with Teen, or feeling suddenly angry (which is often a by-product emotion of loss). Don't be hard on youself; the end of high school is truly the end of an era, and you have the right to mourn its passing for awhile, before a new stage of life emerges for everyone. Where has the time gone? How did he grow to be so tall? Didn't I teach her the alphabet just this morning? And yet, there they are in the auditorium, tassels bobbing, proudly clutching their diplomas, marching to the familiar strain of "Pomp and Circumstance."

"We've only just begun," they tell us. But for us, their parents, the job is nearly over.

Chapter 6

Young Adult:
The Years of Transition

*Children are a lot like kites: You spend a lifetime trying to get
them off the ground . . . Finally they are airborne, but they need
more string and you keep letting it out, and with each twist of the
ball of twine, there is a sadness that goes with the job because the
kite becomes distant, and somehow you know that it won't be long
before that beautiful creature will snap the lifeline that bound you
together and soar as it was meant to soar . . . free and alone.
Only then do you know that you did your job.*
Erma Bombeck

Years ago, with the advent of high school graduation, the child
became an adult. The transition was clear-cut; the dependent
years had ended and our young adult took her place in the
work world, bringing home a salary to help the household. Few
youngsters went on to college, and those who did were either
from extremely wealthy families or else they took classes piece-
meal, dropping out occasionally to earn money for the next
year.

Sometimes a young adult lived at home until marriage; in
those days the extended family comfortably absorbed single
adults of all ages into the household. Family incomes and tasks
were shared, making life more pleasant for everyone, and ban-
ishing much of the loneliness now common both among young
adults and the elderly.

More recently, young adults roamed thousands of miles
away from home in search of a better job, or moved into an
apartment with roommates in order to firmly establish independence. Whatever the method, the delineation was clear, once

the step was taken. The message was: I am an adult.

Today, however, there are no firm boundaries between child and adult. Adulthood, once considered synonymous with independence, has become blurred because of changes in society. More kids do go on to college, remaining financially dependent on parents although they may be mature in many other ways. Those who enter the work world directly from high school soon discover that their salaries can't possibly provide independent living quarters, at least not now. College grads decide to go on for advanced degrees; young marriages crumble and Daughter is left with a baby to support. The job situation is unsettled; young people move hesitantly from position to position, not really sure where they fit. The days of 40-year corporate loyalty seem to be a thing of the past.

In short, today's culture has formed a sort of "transition phase" between the end of high school and the start of adult autonomy. Within that transition phase kids complete their education, flounder around in the work world, make mistakes and continue the learning process. Independence is a struggle, and at times all young adults move forward in one area, backward in another. The twenty-three-year-old grad student may have achieved a high level of intellectual maturity, but he is still not considered an adult because he lacks a credit rating or an annual income. The nineteen-year-old may work capably at a secretarial job, but still demonstrates emotional immaturity in personal relationships. Complete independence is the ultimate goal, but the process is not accomplished easily. It seems to last forever. And in many cases, the young adult opts to live at home while undergoing this transition phase. This decision creates a whole new set of adjustments for both parent and offspring. Sometimes we don't know how to change gears when our sons and daughters grow up, or at least when they enter the transition stage. We go on treating them as children attempting to manage their lives or careers, maintaining overly strict house rules, continuing to do Son's laundry, run his errands, make his dental appointments. While kids who are attempting to dodge adulthood may accept and even welcome this hovering, the average youngster is apt to protest bitterly, and the homefront becomes a battleground, an ongoing struggle for power and dominance.

On the other side are those parents who resent a grownup offspring's continuing presence. Perhaps the earlier parent-teen relationship was rocky and unsatisfying; perhaps parents have a rigid timetable for Son's growth and insist that he now be on his own, even though he's not yet ready for the step. In any case, resentment—unspoken or obvious—can seriously affect the tone of the household. Most parents fall somewhere in the middle. Having come this far on the child-rearing journey, we want to finish the job in the best way possible, by helping our kids through this final transition stage. But we need pointers in order to deal effectively with our new roles. Somehow the relationship must shift completely from one between a dependent child and a decision-making parent to one between a decision-making young person and an accepting parent. Somehow we and our adult children must come together as loving and caring *people*, enjoying each other without the burden of physical or emotional responsibility. How can this change be achieved?

COLLEGE

If your child is college-bound, especially if she will be boarding at school, this move forms a natural transition. For your young adult, college is a way of delaying the full thrust of maturity, yet at the same time adjusting to additional responsibilities. The college student has much to learn about life and about herself. College can be just as educational for parents.

If you're typical, you and Daughter have spent the summer making lists of things she will need for the Big Move. Aside from Girl Scout camp, school trips, or an occasional vacation with friends, she's probably never been away from home before. As you assemble the hot pot, desk lamp, color-coordinated towels and fuzzy new bathrobe (perfect for studying late at night), you worry about whether she'll be able to adjust to this new environment. You don't want to discuss your feelings, though. She may think you're being overly protective or resent your interference.

Go ahead and tell her.

Tell her how natural it is to become homesick, once the initial excitement has died down, and how homesickness can be a debilitating and miserable disease. Tell her that it's something that's got to be faced and worked through, much like a bad case of flu or her first broken heart. She'll feel very proud of herself if she sticks it out, rather than running home at the first twinge and delaying the challenge. Tell her to phone (collect) whenever she's feeling really low; you'll be there to talk it out, to send your love across the wires and into her heart.

Tell her about the difficulties of adjusting to living with strangers, some of whom will never really be her friends. About how it feels to be one of 500 in a lecture hall and how, if she doesn't go in to see the TA (teaching assistant) after class for additional help, no one's going to know or care whether she understood the lesson. About the myriad distractions, everything from laundry to part-time jobs to partying, which will compete for time that should be spent cracking the books. And then tell her that you have confidence in her. Let her know that mistakes are expected, and simply part of the learning process. But no mistake is ever going to dim the love and pride you have in her right now, and always.

Research has shown that the rate of depression and suicide among college students is higher than among the general population. While experts aren't sure exactly why, they do know that college creates pressures that can be overwhelming—*if* the student is not prepared for them. Add to those pressures unreasonably high parental expectations, and the burden can become intolerable. That's why it's important *not* to present a rosy, one-sided portrait of college life. How will your teenager feel if she experiences a totally different picture? Address the normal difficulties she will face as well. In addition, parents must refrain from demanding a certain grade point average, career choice, sorority membership, or other standards as evidence that Teen is a success at school. The student who knows she is loved and valued apart from her achievements or failures, who is realistically prepared for the challenges, will approach campus life in a positive and wholesome way.

So ... you've had your chat with your college-bound teen, the car is loaded down. (How did all that stuff fit in the trunk?) You're off to the campus, and a new life for everyone. Try not to be too shocked at what you find. While the ivy-covered buildings present the same idyllic setting familiar to past generations, a lot has changed since then. There are coed dorms now, and if your daughter lives in one, you'll notice young men wandering around the building clad in jogging shorts (and not much else). Whether your daughter shares a suite with several girls or opts for a tiny single, there will not be enough room—what room there is will be taken up with stuffed animals, small refrigerators and microwave ovens (a collegiate's major hobby is snacking). Married students' quarters are available now, as well as privately-owned off-campus housing for upperclassmen, which is rarely supervised by the college administration. (Naive nineteen-year-olds sign leases without looking at them, and find themselves with no recourse if heat is skimpy or cockroaches abundant.) Part-time job competition is fierce, there are virtually no curfews or personal limitations, all sorts of strange subversive-sounding groups have headquarters on campus and beer seems to be the universal drink. Despite your uneasiness, Daughter will eventually find her way around, discover some compatible pals and learn to organize her time. Trust her—and trust the good foundation you have laid.

(Be sure, however, to caution your daughter about her personal safety, and make her promise that she will not be traveling alone across campus during the dark-and-deserted hours. Rapes or other attacks are no longer unusual on campus, and most universities sponsor an escort service, usually vans driven by male students, to see a coed safely to her dorm from any campus location at any time of night. Daughter will roll her eyes in the typical "that'll never happen to me" gesture you've grown used to seeing, but make her promise anyway. When she sees other coeds taking the threat seriously, she'll do likewise.)

Once home again, you'll have some adjusting to do. Even if you have a large family, the absence of one person does change the flavor of the household, and it takes some getting used to. Her room is so neat; there's still yogurt left in the refrigerator; why doesn't she ever write? (Did you slip some stamped, addressed envelopes in her luggage?) As you begin to relax, however, you also find that you are enjoying the new routine. It's nice to have one less person competing for the bathroom, answering the phone, telling you that you ought to lose weight. Being human, we parents immediately feel guilty about such a reaction, but we needn't; we too are moving into a new phase, the preliminary stages of the empty nest syndrome—and it's natural to enjoy it.

Be sure, however, that you hide such feelings from Daughter when she's home on breaks. Many college kids say they are made to feel like intruders when they are home, people who are obviously interrupting the smooth flow of the household. After a while, some find other places to go for vacations. You don't want this to happen; home is still an important base for collegiates even though their lives are now divided between two residences. It's important that they can count on this security. Besides, how will you otherwise catch up on all the news, since she *still* doesn't write? As your daughter comes back and forth, she'll add a new dimension to your life. Occasionally she'll bring a pal home for the holidays; you'll probably meet them somewhere on the highway, watching with astonishment as they emerge from a car packed with bodies, bags and books. The friend will probably be someone from another part of the country, willing to sleep on the floor, just as nice as your daughter. Invariably she will let a few things slip—and you'll discover that your daughter is dating a wrestler and thinking about switching to Anthropology. Welcome the friend warmly. You will also discover that college isn't divided into a neat four-year curriculum anymore. Few freshmen know exactly what their course of study will be, and as they begin to change their major in sophomore or junior year, several required courses must be made up during summer sessions or a fifth year of schooling. It's also common to drop out of college for a year or so, to work for tuition money or simply to "find oneself," thus further delaying acquisition of the sheepskin.

Some of these tactics are simply a way of delaying independence; but in many cases, kids are genuinely confused about the direction they want to take. If your child does want to finish in four years, however, she'll probably have to settle on a major by the middle of sophomore year, at the latest. Try to impress upon her that her choice isn't written in stone; her degree is only an entry to the job market and once there, she may be trained in a different capacity. "I had a hard time deciding between a math and science major," one graduate reports. "Finally, because I couldn't delay any longer, I settled on engineering. The diploma was enough to get me a job with a large firm that is training me in electronics—something I never considered, although I like it now."

Parents will also find that college phases are a repetition of high school, but on a higher level. Your freshman is timid, hesitant yet willing to experiment and taste deeply of the freedom campus life offers. Kids can easily become overextended during this year. Sophomores are quieter, but many will drop out at this point because they're tired of studying, being poor, or waiting for something to happen. In junior and senior year seriousness prevails; the major field is established, and while confidence is shaky over potential jobs, it's high when handling the college environment. The personality becomes even more integrated, real growth takes place, and your youngster becomes more mature in values, behavior, competence. The transition phase has worked well for her, and at graduation she is ready to assume her place as an adult.

AT HOME

What about the high school graduate who doesn't leave for college or military service, but instead works, perhaps takes a few evening classes, and seems happy to stay at home? He too needs time to find his way, a supportive family environment and the reassurance that it's okay to flounder for a while as he learns and grows. But because he is no longer a dependent child, he does have certain adult obligations, and parents should simply take these obligations for granted. The same rule applies to college grads living at home.

Board—One of these duties (and the one parents seem most confused about) is paying board. No young adult who is working regularly should live at home without contributing some sort of financial payment to the family, whether or not it is needed. To allow a youngster to sidestep this responsibility is to keep him in a dependent and childlike position, and to allow him to take advantage of his folks. Yet many parents are hesitant to impose such a condition. "He's so young ... she isn't earning very much ... he's trying to save for a car ... " are common excuses, and usually mask parental unwillingness to play the heavy or to be unpopular.

And yet haven't we taken difficult stands right along for the ultimate good of the kids? This issue is simply more of the same, and if we do not follow through, we hold our youngsters back from the reality of life. In extreme cases they may still be residing at home at twenty-five or thirty years of age, driving their luxury cars, financing ski trips, and living the Good Life while Mom and Dad keep their clothes laundered and their late dinners warm. Is this the ultimate goal of a parent—for our children and for us?

If not, then the question of paying board has to be addressed as soon as Graduate becomes a wage-earner. The *idea* of board, however, should have been covered much earlier. And it should be approached positively. Board should never be considered a payback for being raised and cared for; parents have no right to financial or emotional reimbursement. Nor should board be considered a gift, something Child bestows out of the goodness of his heart (and which, logically, will become part of a power struggle when he's angry with his parents).

Instead, a parent can say, "Wow, another adult in the house! That's great. Let's figure out how we're going to handle this." And a *very* wise technique is to ask Young Adult what amount of board *she* considers fair. As in other cases, kids are often tougher on themselves than we would ever be.

The amount of board, of course, is going to vary with the youngster and her work conditions. An eighteen-year-old with a minimum-wage job who is trying to save for college will understandably make only a token payment each week. Instead, he can contribute to the family in a nonmonetary way (more about this later). However, an eighteen-year-old who has no interest in college and is instead financing payments on an expensive car is another matter. What are you ultimately teaching this youngster if you allow him to live completely at your expense while indulging himself in luxuries? When the car is paid off, what will be the next item he *must* have, another reason to supersede board?

Sometimes parents waive full board for a short time after a job has been landed, especially for college graduates, in order for Young Adult to use her first few paychecks for a working wardrobe, or a down payment on a modest car. Perhaps a graduate is only planning to live at home for a few months in order to save an apartment security deposit, hookup fees on utilities, etc. In these cases, parents should expect only a small board payment, if any at all, but should be very specific about when this period will end. If Teen hasn't earned what she had hoped by that time and asks for an extension, don't give it. By sheltering her from reality, she avoids learning to cope with the Real World.

Occasionally an older son or daughter may remain home longer than usual because of particular situations. Perhaps your son attends law school full-time, and with a combination of work, grants and loans, he is carrying the burden without any financial help from you. Maybe your daughter expects to finance most of her forthcoming wedding, and she is saving every penny toward this goal. In these cases, you might want to eliminate board in favor of a work arrangement. Although everyone in a family should take on certain chores, whether or not they contribute financially, young adults who are boarding free because of valid circumstances can make an important contribution in other areas. One grad student took over all grocery shopping and dinner preparation for her working mother; such an arrangement fit well with both women's schedules. A young mechanic saving for his wedding completely painted his parents' home and installed a patio during his board-free year at home; both parties felt the barter concept was terrific! Since the ultimate goal is the teen's acceptance of adult responsibility—and since both these young people were behaving responsibly despite financial limitations—the goal had been achieved.

Board needn't cover Junior's entire cost of living at home, but it certainly shouldn't be a token amount either. Handing Mom five or ten dollars a week is as ridiculous as no board at all, especially if Junior is gainfully employed. And it probably shouldn't be a percentage of take-home pay either; such a system seems fair on the surface, since those who earn more pay more, yet it penalizes the youngster who lands the best job. After all, he'll be in a higher tax bracket, too. Many families opt for a weekly payment somewhere around $50, but this can vary greatly depending on wages earned or other circumstances we've discussed. Your working youngster will, of course, also assume responsibility for his medical and dental expenses, clothing, car payment and upkeep, entertainment—in short, all of his expenses. If you are in a position to do so, you may want to help him out from time to time, but remember that this is a *gift*. You have already fulfilled your financial responsibilities to your youngster, and by allowing him to live at home, you are giving him some additional support during this transition phase.

HOUSE RULES

In addition to board, parents often hesitate about making new house rules, now that youngster has passed childhood and adolescence. Is a curfew necessary? After all, Daughter has her own car and is practically supporting herself. Should parents have an input into activities, choice of friends, behavior at home? Or should young adults be able to do anything they please?

"Actually, no rules are necessary for adults if there is consideration," says one mother. "Living together happily and comfortably can only be achieved if everyone thinks of the other guy as well as himself."

Do your young adults phone when they will not be home for supper? Or are you stuck with a six-pound meat loaf and only two or three people to eat it?

Do the kids clean up after midnight pizza and popcorn sessions? Or do you face a sink full of greasy dishes each morning, or worse, a living room disaster area?

Do they do their own laundry? Change their beds? Keep rooms in a semi-orderly state? Pitch in when the lawn needs cutting, a room must be painted? Occasionally phone to put your mind at rest when they are traveling? Or are you considered a personal maid, there just to pick up the pieces?

"If my kids take care of their own business, then I'll stay out of it," one mother explains the motto which has served her well through many years of child-rearing. "Decent manners, consideration, competent management—just handling his own life well proves he doesn't need me sticking my oar into it. Even if he occasionally comes in at 4 a.m., it doesn't bother me—he's proved he's mature enough to handle it."

What if a young adult is *not* tending to business in a grownup way? What if he disrupts the house with angry outbursts, drunkenness or a refusal to help? What if he's over-drawn on his charge accounts and sees no reason why Dad shouldn't bail him out again and again? What if he regards home as a hotel and Mom as a maid service?

"Frankly, some parents allow themselves to be used, even though they gripe about it," says the mother of several young adults. "Maybe their marriage has grown a bit stale, things are dull—and suddenly these lively grownup children come back to roost. Let's face it—they can really pep up a household. And adults are willing to put up with it in order to feel needed again, or to add some pizzazz to their own lives." Parents may also be "stalled" in some point in their own letting-go journey, and are permitting juvenile behavior from their offspring in exchange for keeping the status quo going just a little longer.

Not every household falls into this category, of course. Often we adults are starting a new phase of living at the same time as our children are, and we look forward to a new era of peace, freedom and financial security. If our young adults are not willing to respect *our* rights, then what can we do?

"Give them a choice, pleasantly, of course, but definitely," suggests a father. "They can either shape up and learn some consideration for others (which includes shouldering responsibility for themselves) or they can ship out to a pad of their own, where there's no mandatory dinner hour—and no cook either. It takes self-discipline, this letting go, but to do otherwise is to keep them—and us—in a holding pattern."

"The point is, it is our home," says another dad, "and we parents don't have to put up with any behavior that goes against our moral or social code. It's one thing when a twelve- or thirteen-year-old acts up; he's still a child and discomfort is part of the territory. But any parent who allows an able-bodied young adult to throw his household up for grabs has only himself to blame."

While it's fairly simple to take a stand against drunkenness or an out-of-control temper, what about the young adult who behaves considerately at home, but no longer will attend church, and has apparently given up the early spiritual values his parents took such pains to offer? Your child's rejection of your faith can be a bitter pill to swallow, and it is natural for you to feel like a failure. However, it's important to remember that faith is a journey, not a situation, and everyone must travel this path *alone*, eventually accepting a faith that is "owned," not Mom or Dad's, but mine. Prime searching years seem to be the ages between eighteen and thirty, when young people are addressing many who-am-I? questions. In practical terms, this probably translates into allowing your at-home child to believe the way he wishes, as long as this does not infringe upon your own rights and responsibilities.

For example, if your child refuses to attend church with the family, you may decide to honor his decision, or you may choose to make church attendance a condition for his living at home (so that he will, at least, set an outward example for younger siblings). Pushing your religious beliefs through excessive zeal, shame or angry confrontations will be counter-productive, but you don't need to allow Child to ridicule you either: perhaps a "we won't talk about this subject" stance will be adopted for everyone's sake.

Only you can decide just what kind of an attitude you will take. But don't despair—churches are full of young people who returned when they themselves became parents and had to decide what values to pass on to their own offspring. You have planted the seed of faith; now trust God to help it flourish in His own time.

If kids do decide to live at home responsibly, this period can be a wonderful time for them. Never again will they be so free to involve themselves in other people's lives as helpers and friends. Never again will they have so many hours of leisure activities, self-discovery. Without the time-consuming chores that accompany living alone, they can fill this transition period with marvelous enriching experiences.

THE REVOLVING DOOR SYNDROME

How long should adult children live at home? And what should be done about the increasingly popular "revolving door syndrome"—the adult offspring who moves out, experiences a broken marriage, a quarrel with her apartment mate, an expired lease, and suddenly appears on the doorstep with her suitcases ... and just when you've converted her bedroom into the office you have always wanted?

"This is tricky," advises a parent, "because there may be a valid reason for her reappearance. And you do want to give a troubled offspring some temporary care and help. You don't want to just throw her to the wolves."

"But the key here is 'temporary.'" says another. "You don't want to set up a situation where a child settles in comfortably and expects to share your life—and your refrigerator—on a permanent basis."

Even more sensitive is the situation involving a divorce and grandchildren. Your daughter may definitely need a place to go until she reorders her life and regains some emotional balance. But at your age, are you willing to start raising *her* children?

Most parents suggest that if a child does return to the nest, a definite time limit must be set. "Dad and I will help you care for the children while you look for an apartment and a job ... I know losing a job is difficult, and you can stay here for the next few months until you find another one ..."

"But don't make them too comfortable," cautions a mother who's been through it! "I always told my children that everyone's entitled to *one* mistake, and that we would be here for them to fall back on if that occurred," she says. "But they don't come back as guests. They come for a limited stay. And they don't return a second time."

Such an attitude may seem harsh, but parents can soften the blow in many ways while still making sure that their offspring face up to their roles as adults. "I buy clothes for my grandchildren and occasionally take care of them," says one mother, "but I will not invite my divorced daughter to live with us. Although her life is hard (and it affects me deeply to see her in difficulty), she needs the pride and self-respect that come from meeting these challenges. If she were here, she'd be tempted to sink into dependency again, and she'd lose the growth she's gained from this experience."

"Our twenty-three-year-old son left home somewhat under protest," a father ruefully recalls. "I sensed that he was afraid to cope with being alone—we have a large, close-knit family—but I didn't want him becoming set in a pattern that would be harder and harder to break. He shares an apartment with two other young men now, and because we feel he's still somewhat shaky, we encourage him to drop by regularly. He needs to touch base with us, but he's gradually weaning himself away. And I think he's kind of proud of himself, despite his problems."

In some cases, especially if parents are ill or aged and need a younger person at home, leavetaking may be legitimately delayed. And finances do play a definite role. Many kids absolutely *can't* support themselves on the incomes they currently earn. But ultimately it becomes time to get on with it. True independence can only come when one has left the nest for good.

Make your young adult feel welcome during this important transition period. Be there as an accepting and supportive friend. Let your offspring talk and share, but do not automatically provide answers; don't be outraged when he fails to take your advice. Remain aloof from his business as long as he's coping in the outside world and trying to be considerate at home. Take advantage of the opportunity for shared events—working together on a food pantry, playing golf games, attending concerts, jogging. Remember, this time is special, and it will never come again.

And then, when the moment arrives, let go. Unroll the kite twine as far as it will go, and watch from afar as your youngster soars into his new and independent life.

There will be the inevitable catch in the throat, the worry, the "what if's." But underneath the doubt will be pride, too, the pride that all good parents share. For despite the mistakes, you've done well. You've given your child the best of all gifts—the gift of himself.

Chapter 7

Going it Alone

The best way out of difficulty is through it.

Anon.

Raising teenagers is a complicated business under any circumstances, but it becomes especially challenging when adolescents live in a one-parent household. The custodial parent must grapple with a full-time job in most cases, limits to finances and time, and often personal exhaustion, while also bearing almost complete responsibility for the teen. If adolescence can create trauma in the most stable of two-parent homes, imagine the potential difficulties faced by a mother or dad who must go it alone!

Nor are one-parent families all that rare these days. Current statistics tell us that almost half the children who are now infants will, before age eighteen, live in a single-parent household. Almost one of every four parents will at some time be a single parent. This condition may be temporary, because remarriage is common among those who have lost a spouse through death or divorce. But while it lasts, the one-parent household needs special handling. And if a teenager lives in that household, the custodial parent can expect not only the usual unsettling episodes that surface during adolescence, but also an occasional difficulty stemming directly from the one-parent situation. Single-parent families are by no means automatically inferior to those that include both a father and a mother. The quality of love and care cannot be measured in terms of the number of adults involved. We have all observed two-parent families where the father retreats behind a newspaper, a virtual stranger to his offspring, or the mother, caught up in a career or social rounds, pays only perfunctory attention to the kids. In some two-parent homes, physical or emotional abuse goes on, providing little stability for its members. By contrast, a one-parent home in which love, trust and humor are the cornerstones may be a vastly superior setting, especially for the sensitive teen. Arriving at this peaceful state, however, does take tremendous effort, especially on the part of the custodial parent. But the rewards can be immense.

The principles in this book can be applied to any parent-teen relationship, whether one or both parents are involved. But there may be additional situations for the single parent to handle, simply because she is alone. How are single-parent homes created, and what are the adolescent-related problems that most commonly result?

Death—About 14% of today's one-parent households are caused by the death of a spouse, more commonly the father. And while young fathers do occasionally die, the more familiar scenario involves a man in his late forties or fifties, sometimes dying quite suddenly. A man of this age leaves not only a bereaved wife, but adolescent children as well. Whether death has been sudden or expected, whether the marriage and family life has been rich and full or quite shaky, certain emotions will inevitably stem from this experience. Sadness, anger, guilt, fear and loneliness will touch each family member, and each will have to work through these feelings and come to grips with them. This procedure is called the *grief process*; it's the same normal, healthy, but very painful journey of adjustment you may have already made during different phases of child-rearing and letting-go (although in death, the grief process is more intense than, perhaps, in any other life-change). No two people grieve in quite the same way, and the grief process takes much longer than is commonly realized. These factors, if not understood, can produce additional tension between the surviving spouse and her teens.

Generally, there are three stages in grief. During the first stage, bereaved families function in a state of shock or numbness. The ritual of the funeral, the support of friends, and the myriad details to be handled act as a cushion, protecting survivors from the sorrow that still must be faced.

But the following year or two will probably be the most difficult. Just when outsiders assume that the family is getting over it (and, unfortunately, often start to withdraw support), a widow or widower and the children are beginning to feel the full impact of their loss. There can be a sudden emotional release, weeping and talking endlessly about the loved one. Guilt is common, and so are angry outbursts, in which survivors blame themselves or others, or question their belief in God. Not until the final stage do mourners become reinvolved in life, better able to face the future. Painful episodes still occur, but at less frequent intervals.

If death has been due to a lingering illness, some of this grief process may have started before the final parting. But no matter how leavetaking occurs, professionals claim that grieving *must* be worked through. To avoid it is to delay recovery and perhaps cripple a young person's future relationships.

It's important for a surviving spouse to realize, however, that teenagers do not always grieve in the same manner as adults or small children. Because his emotions are extremely rocky at this time of life, Sixteen may be fearful of expressing sad feelings, lest he lose control completely. Many teens, especially boys, fall into a stiff-upper-lip posture, maintaining a stoic surface, seemingly impossible to penetrate. Others, because they themselves are approaching adulthood, tend to step into the absent parent's role, becoming authoritative with younger siblings or worrying secretly about money; others may become hostile or jealous of intact family structures. If teens are not allowed to work through their grief in natural ways, they may gravitate toward drinking, drugs or daredevil behavior in order to escape their tensions and fears.

Thus, it's important that teenagers be given permission to express sorrow within the family setting. The surviving parent helps them most effectively by her own attitude. Adults should not be ashamed to weep occasionally in front of the kids. Anger is healthy, too; far better for a parent to kick a piece of furniture, hit a wall, or shout "Why did this have to happen?" than to repress such sentiments for the sake of the children. If teens see such emotion expressed, they will feel freer about letting their own feelings out.

As soon as she's able, a surviving parent must also be willing to deal with questions about the future, and to answer them as best she can. Teens in particular want to know about the family financial situation, if Mom will be getting a job or going back to school, how chores will be handled, and other issues affecting their future. But few will ask direct questions; their usual reticence, coupled with an unwillingness to appear unfeeling, will inhibit them—unless Mom takes the initiative. Even if many matters are still unresolved, it's a good idea to hold a Family Council meeting each week, bringing everyone up to date and allowing questions in an open and frank setting. Tears and other emotional outbursts may accompany these meetings, at least for a time, but such exchanges allow the children to become part of the decision-making process and to feel needed and valued.

As the mourning process continues, the surviving parent should not hesitate to talk about the lost spouse from time to time. She may want to give each child a memento of the parent—his watch, his stamp collection or another special token. Far from being morbid, such behavior continues the act of giving permission to grieve, so a teen can more easily continue his own grief process. Knowing that speaking of his dead parent is not off-limits helps him to cope in a more positive way.

Divorce—About 70% of one-parent homes are created by divorce. Current estimates are that more than a third of all children born in the 80's will experience a parental divorce before they graduate from high school. While divorce no longer carries the social stigma that it once did (and can be the absolutely best choice when physical abuse is involved), it is still a devastating experience for many children. Recent studies have shown that, contrary to some opinions, children do not recover easily from this major wrench and, in many cases, carry the trauma into adult life. Further, a child's mental state at the time of the divorce does not necessarily indicate how well she will do later. (Many kids are understandably relieved at the temporary ceasefire that divorce provides, only to later experience a wide range of powerful emotions: anger, fear, bitterness, a sense of failure.) Divorce seem to be the hardest for preteen boys, but problems can be lessened if the boy maintains a good relationship with his father.

If separation takes place when children are very young, they can sometimes be shielded from a divorce's more negative aspects. But teenagers can't, and divorce often leaves them feeling as though the bottom has dropped out of their world. Although teenagers are assumed to be the ones most capable of coping with the breaking up of their homes, the reverse is actually true: the impact of divorce on the already turbulent adolescent stage can cause lasting harm, because this period of a child's life most needs the security of a safety net. Researchers cannot prove a direct link between "non-traditional" families and self-destructive behavior in adolescents. But there has been a parallel rise in divorce and disruptive lifestyles among teens. Kids need stability, and when it's absent, they act out their sense of rejection or fear in dangerous responses—drugs, alcohol, aggressive behavior, abandonment of goals.

It's also a fact that economic pressures will become intense for the custodial spouse (most often, the mother) after the divorce, and will have a negative impact on her teens. A mother's income falls by 73% after a divorce, while Exhusband experiences a gain; sometimes a mother of teens is forced into the workplace after a long period of unemployment, and is unable to provide even the minimum standard of living her children once enjoyed.

Divorcing a mate often means divorcing many people in the family's social support network, as well. Will your former spouse's nieces and nephews still maintain friendly relationships with your teenagers? Will you be forced to move from the family house—and leave behind the neighborhood families who offered much of your children's stability? Your teens may go through a period of loneliness equal to, or even more intense than, your own.

Although it's difficult for separating spouses to concentrate on anything other than their own immediate problems, they can help soften the blow for their teens, even just a little, with the following tactics:

1. Don't keep your marital troubles a secret or deny that problems exist. The kids know it already, and maintaining your credibility now will be important later. It's not necessary (or even healthy) to go into gruesome details or use teenagers as referees or judges, but it can be even more harmful to pretend that everything is fine. Kids whose parents absolutely will not talk to them about personal matters often act out their fear by running away from home, getting into trouble at school or

acting up in other antisocial ways. However painful, straight talk about a family difficulty is best: "Your dad and I are having some problems right now, and we are seeing a counselor to help sort things out. We'll keep you informed."

2. During divorce proceedings, let kids know what changes will be taking place. If Dad is moving out, he should discuss visitation plans with his teens, give them his new address and telephone number, and be careful not to make promises he can't keep. Mom can go over the budget with her teens, and enlist their help and suggestions for keeping the household going. These are difficult moments, and there's no shame in showing anger, sorrow, worry or frustration. A divorce is quite similar to death in terms of the grief journey that everyone will have to make. Both parents should try very hard not to belittle each other in front of the kids; teens in particular need help from *both* parents during this critical growing stage, and nothing will be gained by destroying an adolescent's relationship with one parent or the other. Avoid asking your teen to spy, or carry messages from one parent to the other; it makes him feel guilty and disloyal.

When parents divorce, children often feel that they are to blame. This feeling can be intensified in teens, because they do contribute to the tension in any household, simply by being teens. That's why it's important to reassure them on this point. Let them know that even though Mom and Dad can't live together anymore, each still loves Fifteen and wants to be a continuing part of her life. Dad should attempt to stay in touch, even with letters, phone calls or tapes, if he's a distance away. Visiting arrangements for the nearby Dad can be more casual with teens than with younger children. Encourage Miss Sophomore to drop by whenever she likes. Keep in touch with her at school too; introduce yourself to the principal, ask to be included on the mailing list and participate whenever you can.

Don't worry if visiting day isn't always a big emotional success. Remember, at this stage Dad is an embarrassment to a teen, whether he is divorced or married. She may not want to be seen with you in public; she may not even communicate in more than two-word sentences. Just continue to be there, despite your misgivings, and in time you will see results.

Meanwhile, Mom has an understaffing problem: too much to do, and not enough time, expertise, and hands available. She's exhausted. She begins to share responsibility and authority with her adolescents as near-equals. She tries to be open about her uncertainties, limitations, budget worries. Miss Sixteen often responds by becoming quite independent, mastering skills that her friends couldn't match. Teens from one-parent homes frequently develop strong self-esteem and confidence by learning to manage for themselves, even though they may regret having to do so. They are sometimes so mature that Mom is stunned when they act their age and do something reckless or silly! Mother should be careful now not to nag. It's hard not to overplay the role, especially when she's scared of being alone, but Mom should remember that hers is the only parental voice her teens will hear on a continuing basis. Problems should be discussed as they come up, but nagging can be tremendously disheartening to anyone, especially a teen who is trying to cooperate despite her mistakes.

Never-Marrieds—About 10% of single parents have never been married. Some of these had infants out of wedlock and have raised them alone; another segment has gone through single-parent adoption, occasionally taking an older child into the home. This group differs from parents affected by death or divorce in that there is no grief to be worked through with one's teen, no upheaval or trauma due to loss. However, kids whose parent has died or divorced did at one time live with two parents. Even if the relationship was rocky or distant, they have had the benefit of relating to both sexes. Not so the teenage children of never-married parents. It's to be hoped that such offspring have always had opportunities for relationships with adults of both sexes who acted as warm and caring role models. But if such has not been the case, a single parent should make a special effort for her emerging adolescent. Parents Without Partners and Big Brothers or Big Sisters of America are groups that provide friends for kids from one-parent families, giving Fourteen the chance to ask questions, share activities, blow off steam or just *talk*—especially important at those times when he can't seem to get through to his own Mom or Dad. Offspring of never-married parents sometimes face a social stigma too: rude questions from pals, occasional sneers or name-calling regarding Sixteen's origins. While you've probably handled this situation before, be vigilant about its recurrence during the teen years. Teens have a horror of being different from their peers, and a boy who has never had a father (even though he happily accepted the situation for years) may now feel very vulnerable about it. Be sure to reassure him that he is dearly loved and cherished; as his natural mother, you could have aborted him or given him away; as his adopted mother, your life has been immeasurably enriched because of his presence. Such messages should be a constant part of a child's upbringing, and if you haven't discussed the matter in several years, bring it up again. Chances are, Son will mumble or stare at the ceiling. But he'll get your message.

Parents who raise teenagers alone run into the same stumbling blocks that their married counterparts do. But in the absence of a partner, some of these conflicts can be more difficult to solve. Others may be influenced by your single role. Let's look at each relationship, and the most common situations that result.

Mother-Daughter—There is a special bond that exists between mothers and daughters which can ripen into a warm and rewarding friendship. This closeness does not usually occur during the teen years, though. Your daughter draws away from you now precisely *because* she has felt so close to you before. She needs to make it on her own, to feel confident about herself before she can allow the two of you to become friends—and equals—again.

Because a girl becomes estranged from her mother during adolescence, the normal romantic feelings she had for her dad during the preschool years sometimes resurface. As a result, she may again go through some resentment over the divorce; she might even blame you for "driving Daddy away." In extreme cases, she may create problems in the hope of being allowed to live with Dad. This is tough to take, but you must guard against falling into the trap of bad-mouthing your ex-spouse, dredging up old wounds, or becoming hostile, thus giving your out-of-bounds daughter more ammunition to use against you. If the situation warrants it, you can consider giving custody to your ex, but don't do it out of spite or retaliation toward him or your daughter. You want to keep the lines of communication open so that in later years, your daughter will want to rebuild her relationship with you.

If you continue to raise your daughter, try to show respect for her individuality. As a single mother, it's far too easy to become domineering, to want for your daughter what you didn't have and to try to control her life toward this end. Some girls, aware that "Mom is all I have," may slip into submission through fear. Others will rebel, often using unsuitable dating partners or unsavory activities as wedges. They're saying, "See, you can't control me!" In either case, the message is clear: your daughter is not you, and she has a right to grow in her own way.

A certain amount of competitiveness is also normal in the mother-daughter relationship, and may intensify when Mom is the only parent. Some of this is caused by Mom's misgivings about growing older, perhaps feeling like a failure in the midst of a divorce. But Daughter often feels that she has a lot to live up to! She sees you making it, holding down a job, keeping a family together, perhaps involved in social activities—confident and cool—and that's a hard act to follow. Will she be able to handle her adult life with the same degree of skill and competence? Never mind that you don't *feel* confident and cool—your daughter sees you that way. Her uncertainty is often exposed in her criticism of you. She's attempting to tear you down so she won't have so much to live up to.

Try to see to it that your daughter receives adequate training for a career. Discuss your own situation with her, and let her know how important it is for women to be selfsufficient. As for the rest, try to stay calm—and love her. This difficult period won't last forever.

Father-Daughter—Whether Dad is raising his daughter or only sees her sporadically, her teenage blooming catches him unaware. He and she both become somewhat sensitive and hesitant about the horseplay, tickling and rough-housing of the past. Eventually they move together into a new, more mature relationship.

The transformation is not accomplished easily. Some dads become anxious over Daughter's emerging sexuality and attempt to quell it with crossness or even cruelty. Others deny it, forbidding Daughter to date, attempting to continue the past relationship in the same way, trying to keep her Daddy's little girl forever. Others, disappointed in their wives, form especially deep alliances with their daughters, many of whom may catch the signals and play Papa for all he is worth.

None of this behavior is fair to a girl. She needs dependability in her father, but not his dependency. She has a right to receive warmth and tenderness from him, but Dad should *not* respond to her flirting or seductive behavior. Nor should Dad slip into apathy. An uncaring or hostile father sometimes is the reason why girls gravitate into promiscuity. They desperately need to feel valued by males, and have nowhere else to look.

This fine line is difficult for a father to walk, especially if you are the non-custodial parent. Things would be more natural if you saw Daughter at home every day in a less contrived setting. However, you must try. Remember that your daughter's primary need is security; she wants to know that you love her, are proud of her, like to spend time with her and won't ever abandon her emotionally. While it might be difficult to put your feelings into words, you can supply her need simply by being there in as many ways as you can. Go to her piano recital, take her out for lunch, give her a hug, send her a funny card. Don't avoid events just because you might meet your ex-wife there. A little social embarrassment is a small price to pay to support your daughter on a big occasion. Don't be overly indulgent with gifts or the granting of unreasonable requests—don't allow Daughter to manipulate you—but do give her a special treat from time to time. Guard against letting her play one parent against the other. Pointing out your ex's good qualities occasionally will aid your daughter's emotional well-being a lot more than tearing Mom to pieces. Try, too, to take part in discussions with your daughter over personal subjects which are dear to her heart, though they may seem tedious to you—things like dating, dress codes, values, even what she like to do on weekends. Such discussions set the tone for a more intimate relationship, and make Daughter feel secure and loved.

Don't worry if you feel a bit awkward with your daughter. She is, after all, growing up, and the relationship will not be quite the same as it once was. Even so, what you want is a closeness that will last into her adult years, and this will not be easy if you are constantly judgmental, critical, or argumentative.

Daughter will not be able to communicate as well as you would like, either, especially now when sensitivity is at its peak in her. Despite these problems, try and try again. She's well worth it.

Mother-Son—Adolescent boys are a bit easier for single mothers to raise than girls. A boy is not going through a competitive phase with Mom, isn't trying quite as hard as his sister to discredit her. On the other hand, boys in female-dominated homes will struggle hard for their independence, and a mother often feels overwhelmed when her little guy gets large. How can she handle him now, especially when he's yelling at her, without a man around?

The key here is to *request*, not demand. If your son has been your junior partner for years, helpful and willing to shoulder burdens for you, it's unfair to expect him to bow to arbitrary demands now, simply because he is now a teen and you *need* his help. Rather than imposing rules of conduct, discuss them in family councils and see if you can compromise. A son who has been decent and loving prior to adolescence is not going to turn into a monster just because he has started high school. Keep talking with him and expressing your faith in his good judgment. Step in when you must, but don't anticipate problems just because you are a one-parent family.

Some single mothers feel rather inept in the male culture, and guiltily believe that they are depriving their sons because of an absent father. They tend to idealize two-parent homes, forgetting that plenty of fathers in intact families don't take any meaningful part in their sons' lives. While it is true that your son would enjoy and benefit from playing sports, tinkering with cars and other male pursuits, he can certainly share such time with a grandfather, uncle or other male role model. Many boys *with* fathers do the same thing. Try to find substitute male figures for your son; if he has the chance to develop lots of male relationships, with ministers, teachers, neighbors or coaches, they will provide balance for him. Occasionally a mother will attempt to model her son into the type of man she wishes her husband had been, or pattern him after an adored deceased father. Such boys are expected to pay homage to Mom, act as an escort or confidant and, in extreme cases, avoid entanglements with women their own age. Most boys, despite a desire to please Mom and compensate for her loss, will eventually rebel at these expectations—and they should. Your son has a right to follow his own path. Believe in his potential, but don't try to make him live out your dreams.

Mom should also avoid giving Son too much responsibility, attempting to make him the Man of the House. A teenage boy often takes on the role of rescuer for his single mother; he loves her and doesn't want to create family crises, so he avoids burdening her with his problems or assumes roles he's really not ready to handle. However, such an overload can exhaust him, and that's one of the reasons why boys often ask to live with their dads during their teen years. You should enlist your son's cooperation and help where you feel you must—for household chores and the like—but don't make him into a substitute peer or parent for younger siblings. He needs time to mature in his own way.

Father-Son—It has been said that when a son stops fearing his father, he has become a man. And this is the job of an adolescent boy: to break away from hero-worship, to risk his dad's displeasure again and again (even in minor matters), to establish a separate identity—and only then to come full circle as a lifelong friend. While most fathers understand this process, having gone through it themselves, they tend to be far less tolerant of their own sons than they would be if some other boy was doing the same thing. Many dads become authoritative and critical, playing the heavy whenever Son is involved in a minor escapade. Others, because of laziness or confusion (or, in the case of a divorced father, the fear of losing Teen's company), forfeit leadership and slip into apathy or permissiveness.

Since in the majority of divorces, Dad is the noncustodial parent, communication between father and son will be even more difficult. Men tend to talk on an impersonal level. They can't seem to have it out with the same ease that mothers and sons do. And there is the factor of expectation too. A father often dreams about a son following in his career footsteps, or making a name for himself on the football field, in science or medicine. Such hopes often collide with reality when a teen steps out of the mold and rejects his father's plans. All of these irritations can seem even more intense to a father who is distanced from his son, and can't deal with him on a daily basis.

As in the case with daughters, Dad must be sure to show his

acceptance of his son as he *is*, while caring enough to discipline him when the situation calls for it. If words are hard to find, a father can show indirect interest—casting a proud glance, retelling Son's triumph within Son's earshot, asking an interested question (and avoiding responding with a lecture), simply giving a pat on the shoulder. Times together can be casual. Even cleaning up your apartment or cooking a meal in tandem can be a lesson in nonsexist behavior between father and son, helping to break down the stereotype of "woman's work," and teaching your son a broader role.

This will not be the only example you set for Son; if you are given custody, for example, you'll have to make important career decisions—you cannot work until 10 p.m. and expect Teen to come home from school, do his homework, make dinner and arrange a ride to and from an evening school function or job. This is worse than no custody at all—and gives Son a loud message: things and positions are more important than kids. (You may not believe this at all, but it's the message your neglected boy will receive.)

Boys often receive a severe jolt when their fathers begin to date again after being widowed or divorced. They register shock that old over-the-hill non-sexual *Dad* can have a relationship with a *woman*, similar to their own relationships. It doesn't make sense. Part of their reaction is also rooted in *envy*. Like the daughter who secretly admires her mother, while never missing a chance to tear her down, a boy feels at a competitive disadvantage with a male parent who is so much more sophisticated in the art of romance. Then too, if a boy has been especially fond of his mother, Dad's dating will be seen as an act of disloyalty. Fathers must have the opportunity to rebuild their own lives, but they must be especially sensitive to the reactions of their teens when another woman becomes part of the picture. While some experts downplay the negative aspects of live-in or sleep-over partners, a father should be very careful about introducing this situation into his life. Adolescents hold parents to fairly stringent moral standards. They're developing their own moral codes, and they can be especially critical of parental failings. And it is absolutely hypocritical for a father to live by one standard while expecting his son to adhere to another.

Fathers often underestimate their importance to their children. They see kids as physical extensions of wives, and as parents alone they feel excluded and incapable. Worse, they're trained to believe that raising children is primarily a woman's job because she's better at it. And yet nurturing really isn't gender-related. A father is a powerful factor in a child's emotional growth, whether he wants to be or not. He serves as a role model for his sons, reassuring them about themselves in ways that their mother never could. He serves as the first love interest in his daughter's life, making an impact on how she will later relate to men. Dad must be there for his teenage kids—physically if possible, but even more important, emotionally, whether single or married. No one else will love those children in quite the way that he can. Single parenting—not the easiest way to raise teens, not the route that many might have chosen. But with talk, tenderness, and outside support, it can definitely work.

STEP-PARENTING

"I thought it would be just the two of us," fifteen-year-old Eileen told a counselor shortly after her divorced mother had remarried a man with two young boys. "I already had a father—I didn't need another one. And I *sure* didn't need two bratty stepbrothers to mess up my life even more!" Although Eileen eventually reached a shaky armistice with her new step-family, it wasn't an easy process—and at times, both she and her mother despaired of ever being friends again.

Divorced moms and dads seldom realize how hard it is for their children when they remarry. Typically, Eileen lost privacy, attention, her position as an "only child" and even a larger share of the household income. Because her blended family moved to a new location, she lost her familiar classrooms and teachers, old friends, the security of her bedroom and her household routines. Worst of all, she lost the (sometimes unconscious) dream that almost all children of divorce nurture: that her mother and father might someday reunite, and live happily ever after. Seeing a parent marry someone else, no matter how nice a person in his/her own right, is probably the most devastating loss any young person can sustain.

In addition, because teenagers have a longer history of loyalty to a biological mom or dad, they have a much more difficult time going through this mourning process and eventually accepting a stepparent than younger siblings do. One study found that the worst time for adults to remarry was when children were between the ages of nine and fifteen, because these were the years when kids struggled most for independence, and most resented an "outsider" attempting to get involved in their lives and tell them what to do. (By contrast, eighteen- or nineteen-year-olds sometimes welcome a remarriage, because it relieves them of feeling responsible for their custodial parent's loneliness once they leave for college or their own apartments.)

According to experts, the early blended-family stages are usually the worst, because both boys and girls are mad at their parent for remarrying, and determined to be hostile, sulk, or do whatever they can to sabotage the new relationship. A girl seems to have a harder time accepting it all; she experiences the most stress if it's a stepfather that's involved—and even after a few years, may resent his attempts to be authoritative or affectionate. Girls have trouble relating to a stepmother too; the "other woman" is not only a rival with Mom, but competition for Daddy's love and attention for Daughter.

Boys fare a bit better; if stepdads go slowly and build family ties one day at a time, boys can be open to the changes. And although a boy may feel extremely hostile to a new stepmother, he often masks this with withdrawal or other more socially acceptable attitudes. As time passes, such surface neutrality may actually change to something resembling pleasantness.

If you are remarrying, consider the following steps. They may make blended-family adjustments easier for everyone involved.

• Prepare your children for the change. "It's amazing," says a counselor, "but many parents simply get married one day, and expect the kids to accept everything happily." While your decision to marry is your own—and you don't need "permission" from offspring of any age—it is not only wise but compassionate to involve your children in your wedding ceremony (if they are willing) and other plans long before they happen. While he will probably be unhappy about the situation, he will also benefit from time to get used to the idea.

• Discuss your methods of parenting with your new spouse

before your marriage. Get down to basics on questions such as: How will we spend leisure time? What will we do if one of us doesn't approve of the other's discipline methods? What do we allow our children to say or do? What are our priorities, the things we absolutely can't compromise with the kids about? Ambivalence over these issues lets a perceptive teen know that no one is in charge, and that she can easily play one adult off the other to get whatever she wants.

Consider setting up a weekly family meeting even before your wedding, and keep it going afterwards. Involve all the children, but especially adolescents, who usually have very definite ideas of how things should be done. Give them the chance to vent as well as the responsibility for certain chores; keep asking for feedback the following week and don't be afraid to experiment. This process helps kids understand that responsibility for making us a family belongs to all of us. (If teens refuse to attend family meetings, don't push; it will be obvious to everyone else that Teen is not making the effort necessary to communicate, so how can Step-Dad be blamed for not understanding him?)

• Make your new marriage your priority. This seems obvious, but after some weddings, the new home becomes simply a pit-stop, a place to grab whatever one needs—food, rest, sex—on the way to someplace else. When Norma remarried, for example, she was already working full-time to help support her two daughters, then ages eleven and thirteen. Norma kept her job, in order to meet payments on the large suburban house she and her new husband bought, and a short time later, her company offered to cover the cost of her going back to college for her master's degree. Thrilled, Norma accepted. It was less than two years before this fragile family crumbled, more from a lack of commitment than from any major deficiencies. Norma had failed to put her new marriage first, to give both her husband and her daughters a sense of continuity and security by simply being *there* for all of them. Deprived of the time to learn to relate to one another, no one did.

• Don't try too hard. Studies show that men, especially if they have never been parents before, tend to "come on" a bit too hearty with their stepchildren, perhaps in the mistaken idea that the kids need a strong role model and they must fill those shoes. Actually, what the kids need most, at least as a blended family originally forms, is some emotional support and friend-ship. Men who behave pleasantly with children of both sexes, take time to talk reasonably with them and even ask their opinions, are probably breaking the ice in the best possible way under the circumstances. It's probably best for stepfathers to avoid too much hugging or caressing—it can easily be misinterpreted, especially from touchy teens—and to concentrate on verbal praise. Later on, when relationships are closer, stepfathers can take a more disciplinary role and teens will accept it.

Such advice is also prudent for stepmothers who, because women are expected to be nurturing, often try too hard to become parent figures and wind up antagonizing their husband's children instead. It's best to avoid competition with the kids' mother under any circumstances, and instead, to aim for a role as friend and mentor. You should run the household in the most comfortable ways for you (you are the housemom after all, even if you're not the kids' mom), and refuse to apologize for the way you are; but you should also remember that a smile, a compliment (and sometimes a deaf ear) go a long way. With time, your husband's children may regard you as a very special person, someone they would have hated to miss. And you'll feel the very same way.

Chapter 8

The Fine Art of Negotiating

*All government—indeed, every human benefit and
enjoyment, every virtue and every prudent act—
is founded on compromise and barter.*
Edmund Burke, 1795

Throughout the teen years, agreements must be reached (or at
least attempted) on various subjects. Some families can handle
these issues verbally, simply sitting around the kitchen table
from time to time, discussing the pros and cons, then reaching a
plan that is pleasing to everyone. Other families can't talk well
together, at least not during the adolescent years. Teens can be
closed-mouthed, parents too quick to jump to conclusions. Emotions which are rooted in unrelated experiences can erupt and
cloud the issue at hand. Communication sometimes is misun-
derstood, too: Parent said one thing but thought he meant
something else; the teenager interpreted a remark her way instead of the way it was intended. And occasionally, both parties
forget the terms of the agreement after time passes by. For these
reasons, some parents prefer to draw up contracts which spell
everything out in unmistakable terms. Teens can add their own
points to these contracts too. As in the real legal world, if both
parties sign the contract, then both are bound by its terms. If
only one party is willing to sign, or if both sign and one later de-
faults by not living up to the terms, the contract is null and void.
Penalties for defaulting should always be clearly spelled out in
the contract.

Contracts are a novel way to help build trust between family members. Even though parents have authority over their off-spring, they should take a contract seriously and live up to its terms, just as they expect their teens to do. Teens, in turn, have a real opportunity to prove their maturity. If they fail to honor the contract, they can't beef when privileges are withheld. Fair is fair. Even a teen will admit that!

Let's take a look at a few contracts that real families have drawn up. In each case, the stipulations were debated before being included. Teens in the families had some input. The contracts were intended not only to set up the rules of play, but also as a teaching device, to help teens grow and learn.

ALLOWANCES

The following agreement was devised by parents who wanted to help their son budget his money, and also to be responsible for buying some of his own necessities. He was receiving an allowance and earning a sporadic income by shoveling snow and cutting lawns. He spent both immediately on frivolous items, and had fallen into the habit of begging for loans, which were never repaid.

Date _____

We, *John and Wilma White*, agree to pay our son, *Tim White, age 14*, the sum of *$7.50* on Friday evening of each week, for the year of 19___, according to the following terms:

A. Not less than $1.00 of the $7.50 per week shall be set aside in a savings account.

B. Not less than fifty cents of the $7.50 per week shall be set aside to cover all school supplies, excluding textbooks.

From the remaining allowance combined with outside earnings, Tim shall be required to purchase:

A. All haircuts at maximum three-month intervals.

B. Three pairs of gym and/or dress shoes during the next calendar year, as needed.

C. All gifts to be given family members and friends for birthdays, Christmas and other occasions.

D. Lunch at school, if home-packed bags are refused.

Tim is given the right to spend all remaining income at his own discretion. No loans or additional income will be provided by parents under any circumstances.

Forfeiture:

1. If Tim fails to live up to the above terms, his allowance will be terminated. No loans or additional income will be provided by parents.

2. If parents fail to provide Tim with the specified allowance at the specified time, the amount owed Tim will double.

Signed_____(Date)

Signed_____(Date)

STUDY SCHEDULES

The parents of a high school sophomore became concerned when his grades, previously high, began slipping. They realized that he was happily involved in several wholesome extracurricular activities, and was developing a satisfying social life, and they didn't want to curtail these pleasures. But they believed his first priority had to be schoolwork.

Their son saw no reason why he should limit evening club meetings or telephone conversations with his friends. His "C" average seemed adequate, and besides, he had more interesting things to do! Together they decided to compromise:

Date _____

We the undersigned are accepting this contract for the semester beginning _____ and ending _____. During this time:

1. Telephone calls, socializing, club meetings and other recreational activities will be permitted for Paul each weekday up until 8 p.m. and throughout the weekend.

2. Paul will spend the hours from 8 to 10 p.m. each Sunday through Thursday (see #3) in his room doing homework. During these hours, no telephone conversations or TV watching will be allowed. Parents will answer Paul's calls, and inform friends of the rule. If Paul has no homework, he will still spend this time in his room in "quiet pursuits."

3. Paul will be permitted one (1) weeknight out each week for club meeting only (no socializing), and *only* if homework has been completed before the meeting. If homework has not been completed prior to the meeting, Paul will not attend.

At the end of the semester, Paul's report card will be evaluated. If his grade point average has improved, this contract will remain in force for the next semester. If his grade point average remains the same or slips, Paul will forfeit his extracurricular activities during the following semester.

Signed _____ (Date)
Signed _____ (Date)
Signed _____ (Date)

LOANS

An eighteen-year-old high school graduate wanted to purchase a used car, but she had been working for such a short time that she had saved no money. Her father, wanting to spare her high interest rates and teach her how to handle monthly payments promptly, agreed to lend her the money under the following circumstances:

Date _____

I, *James Kelly*, agree to lend *Nora Kelly* the amount of *$2400* at *no* interest for the purchase of a car. The $2400 shall be paid back on the *1st* day of each month at a rate of *$100* each month, commencing on _____ (Date) for the next *24* months. Title shall remain in the name of James Kelly until debt has been satisfied. Nora Kelly has the option of repaying the loan at a faster rate than the above terms specify.

Forfeiture:

Should the payment be late, a penalty of $5.00 per day for each day's delinquency shall be added to the monthly payment. Should payment be more than three months in arrears, James Kelly shall exercise his right of title and sell the car for the recovery of outstanding debt.

Signed _____ (Date)

Signed _____ (Date)

CAR USE

Preparing to earn his driver's license, a sixteen-year-old asked his parents when and under what conditions he would be allowed to drive the family car. He was also thinking about using his job earnings to purchase a car of his own, something his parents were very much opposed to at this time. After several discussions, a solution was agreed upon by all:

Date _____

We, *Mark and Sara Claybourne*, parents of *David, age 16*, do hereby draw up conditions for David's use of the second family car for the period covering 19___ to 19___ (approximately two years):

1. David will be required to pay his portion of the auto insurance carried by the family, such payment being due on *January 1* and *July 1* of each calendar year, and in the amount of $125 per payment, subject to rate change by the insurance company.

2. David will be required to keep track of his personal mileage in the enclosed notebook, and will provide gasoline in the amount of one gallon per ten miles, payable on a weekly basis.

3. David will be responsible for checking air in the tires, maintaining fluid levels and oil changes for the second car at the appropriate times; these and other maintenance costs will be covered by parents.

4. David will drive carefully, obey the rules of the road and act responsibly at all times.

5. David will inform parents where he is driving the car, whom he is with and what time he will return.

6. At termination of this contract (David's 18th birthday), negotiations will begin concerning David's purchase of a car of his own.

Forfeiture:

If any of the above conditions are not met, or if David receives more than one traffic citation, or if he is involved in a chargeable traffic accident, or if he at any time drives under the influence of alcohol or drugs, he will surrender his driving privilege for a period of not less than *two months*. In return, Mark and Sara Claybourne agree to provide the second family car for David's use every Friday evening, during Wednesday and Thursday after-school hours for work purposes, and at other times if convenient for all, except in cases of extreme family emergency. Should Mark and Sara Claybourne fail to live up to the above agreement, David shall be entitled to purchase a car of his own before his 18th birthday.

Signed _____ (Date)

Signed _____ (Date)

HOUSEHOLD CHORES

A single mother and her teenage daughter were at sword's point over the matter of chores and babysitting duties for a younger brother. Mom needed help, but Daughter complained that she was too often expected to fill in on a moment's notice, after she had already made plans of her own. Mom had begun to nag, and Daughter was retaliating by refusing to do even the most minimal of housework. Together they eventually decided on the following:

Date _____

We, *Andrea and Susan Miller*, do hereby agree on the following terms regarding chores and babysitting duties:

Part One
A. Susan will be responsible for the complete care of her clothing, including all laundry, ironing, mending and dry cleaning.

B. Susan will cook the family dinner on Monday, Tuesday and Wednesday evenings each week, following the menu that Andrea has provided.

C. Susan will assist in general apartment cleanup on Saturday mornings between the hours of 11:00 and 12:30.

D. Susan will babysit for her brother, Jeff, during occasional weekday evening hours, *provided* that Andrea's request for such babysitting service be made no later than Sunday evening each week; such requests not to exceed two evenings per week.

Forfeiture:
If the above conditions are not met, Susan forfeits her allowance and the use of the family car.

Part Two

A. Andrea agrees to be responsible for all additional household chores and errands not covered above.

B. Andrea agrees to provide all weekend babysitters for Jeff, and all weekday services not covered above, when necessary.

C. Andrea will continue to provide both allowance and access to the family car for Susan.

Forfeiture:

If the above conditions are not met, Susan is excused from the obligations outlined in Part One.

Signed _____ (Date)

Signed _____ (Date)

DATING RULES

A seventeen-year-old girl was tired of being grilled by her parents before each date; she felt their questions indicated a lack of trust in her. Her parents wanted to be sure she would be safe and was not going to objectionable places. Here's the way they compromised:

Date _____

We the undersigned agree to the following conditions involving Carol's weekend dating privileges:

A. Carol may choose any dating partner she wishes without prior consultation with parents, unless parents have information regarding such partner's bad reputation with regard to drinking and drugs. If such information is valid, Carol will refrain from dating this partner.

B. Carol may make her own social arrangements, providing she willingly and truthfully

1. Informs parents of where she will be going and who she will be with,

2. Informs parents of the approximate time of her return. Within reason, curfew hours will be left to Carol's discretion. If she has not arrived home at this time, she will phone home and explain. If such information is forthcoming and candid, parents agree not to probe for more information.

C. Carol may choose her own mode of dress for dating, providing such attire is of a modest nature; if disagreements arise between Carol and her father over dress, her mother will be the final arbiter.

D. Carol's conduct on dates will be trustworthy and moral; the use of alcohol and drugs is strictly forbidden.

Forfeiture:

Should Carol violate any of the above clauses, her dating privileges will be suspended for a period of not less than one month.

Signed _____ (Date)

Signed _____ (Date)

ROOMMATE RULES

This brief contract was not negotiated by parents—they had thrown up their hands in despair over the problem—but between two teenage sisters who shared a bedroom. The elder, Lisa, was organized and meticulous, and resented sharing living quarters with her sloppy and careless sister. The younger, Julie, was sick of being nagged over the disorder, but she also envied her sister's larger wardrobe and wanted to borrow clothes on occasion. Lisa seized upon Julie's "weak spot" and the two reached an agreement that satisfied both of them:

Date _____

I, *Julie*, promise to help Lisa clean our bedroom every Sunday night. During the week I promise to put my dirty laundry into the hamper each night, bring my dirty dishes to the kitchen each morning and keep papers off the floor.

I, *Lisa*, promise to stop nagging Julie about disorder *other* than that covered above. If she remains faithful to her promise, I will let her borrow two or three items of my clothing or jewelry each week . . .

provided she asks first, and

provided said articles are returned to me in the same condition as they were lent.

No cleaning, no lending.

Signed _____ (Date)
Signed _____ (Date)

BATHROOM USE

Finally, a frustrated parent who was tired of his sons' constant use of the bathroom, posted this tongue-in-cheek message on the door:

I, the Head of Household, being temporarily of unsound mind, do hereby declare that henceforth:

1. All showers be no more than five minutes in length.

2. No more than two (2) daily showers per person will be permitted.

3. No more than one (1) daily shampoo per person will be permitted.

4. No more than three (3) towels per week per person will be permitted.

5. Said bathroom shall be cleaned each Saturday morning by users on a rotating basis.

If such conditions are not met:

1. All soap, towels, shampoo and hair dryers will be confiscated and held for ransom under lock and key.

2. Water supply will be turned off at its source by aforementioned Head of Household.

Proclaimed this _____ day of _____, 19___.

While this is not a contract in the strict sense of the word, it's said the proclamation led to a dramatic drop in this household's water bill.

Chapter 9

Help is a Four-Letter Word, Too

There are times when every good parent needs and deserves help—and there's no disgrace in taking advantage of it. The following listings may provide just what you're looking for!

GENERAL INTEREST BOOKS

Available in most libraries.

The Birth Order Book, Kevin Leman, Ph.D., Fleming Revell, 1985. An intriguing in-depth study of birth order; both parents and adolescents will find much of interest here.

Drug-Proof Your Kids, Steve Arterburn and Jim Burns, Focus on the Family Publishing, Pomona CA 91799, 1989. Dial toll-free 1-800-A-FAMILY for ordering information on this and many other parenting resources.

Getting From Twenty to Thirty, Mike Edelhart, M. Evans & Co., 1983. Divided into three interesting sections: Breaking away from one's family, Remaking one's world, and Arriving there in one piece. Upbeat and helpful for the post-adolescent.

Help! Harper and Row Publishers, Inc., Icehouse One-401, 151 Union St., San Francisco CA 94111 $3.95. Handbook dealing with problems such as peer pressure, failure in school and curfews.

Helping Your Teenager Deal with Stress, Bettie B. Youngs, J.P.

Tarcher, 1986. Tips parents can use to recognize and diminish their youngsters' stress levels.

Kids, Drugs and Alcohol, A Parent's Guide to Prevention and Intervention, Anne Swany Harrity/Ann Brey Christensen, Betterway Publications, 1987. An excellent guide to the current drug scene, offering practical suggestions for prevention, early detection and intervention.

A Parent's Guide to Letting Go, Betty Fish, M.S.W. and Raymond Fish, Ph.D., M.D., Betterway Publications, 1988. Discusses transitions that *parents* must go through, in order to separate fully from their children and learn more about themselves in the process.

The Parents' Guide to Teenagers, edited by Leonard Gross, Macmillan Publishing Co., 1981. Gross has gathered the opinions of over 300 teen authorities into this work. The medical, psychological and educational communities address questions ranging from brother-and-sister relationships to loneliness to juvenile diabetes. Little in-depth treatment here, but an excellent overview.

Parents and Teenagers: Getting Through to Each Other, Margaret Albrecht, Parents' Magazine Press, NY, 1972. A helpful study of the generation gap, with the suggestion that parents may learn as much from their children as they teach!

Preparing for Adolescence, James C. Dobson, Ph.D., Bantam Books, 1978. This well-known psychologist and founder of Focus on the Family, a support network for parents, addresses tricky issues with clarity and wisdom.

Smart Kids, Stupid Choices, Kevin Leman, Ph.D., Regal Books, 1987. Explanations of the pressures teens face today and how they learn to make the right decisions.

Step-by-Stepparenting, A Guide to Successful Living with a Blended Family, James D. Eckler, Betterway Publications, 1988. A divorced and remarried Baptist minister offers guidelines for making blended families successful and loving.

Surviving an Eating Disorder, Michele Siegel, Judith Brisman and

Margot Weinshal, Harper & Row, 1988. New hope for what has been called the "anxiety disease."

Welcome to The Real World, Annie Moldafsky, Doubleday (Dolphin) 1979. This book is actually written for young adults, but it can be an eye-opener for parents, too, because it deals with issues and feelings confronting kids as they start life on their own.

When Teenagers Work: The Psychological and Social Cost of Adolescent Employment, Ellen Greenberger and Laurence Steinberg, Basic Books, 1986. Heavily researched and somewhat negative, this book still offers much food for parental thought about teenage work commitments.

Why You Feel Down and What You Can Do About It, Irma and Arthur Myers, Charles Scribner's Sons, 1982. Written by a psychotherapist, this work examines teen depression, helps teenagers (and parents) understand their problems, and encourages adults to hold firm on their value system.

BOOKS FOR STUDENTS BOUND FOR COLLEGES AND TECHNICAL SCHOOLS (AND THEIR FOLKS)

Available in libraries and through high school guidance offices.

Peterson's Four Year Colleges and *Peterson's Two-Year Colleges*, Princeton, NJ (updated each year). These offer just about all the information high school juniors need to narrow their search for just the right college. Fat reference books are at-a-glance directories that match your preferences, budget and geographical interests with colleges, and include a listing of over 100 college videos available for home use.

Insiders' Guide to the Colleges, compiled by the staff of the *Yale Daily News*, St. Martin's Press (updated each year). Students tell what the 300 colleges listed are *really* like. An interesting and witty read, with plenty of practical information.

College Cost Book, $10.95 to College Board, Box 886, New York NY 10101. Lists costs for over 3100 colleges, as well as step-by-step advice on applying for financial aid.

Handbook of Trade and Technical Careers and Training, National Association of Trade and Technical Schools, 2021 K Street N.W., Washington, DC 20006

How and Where to Get Scholarships and Financial Aid for College, R. L. Bailey, Arco Publishing.

Need a Lift? The American Legion, Department SPO, Box 1055, Indianapolis, IN 46202. $1.00 ppd., revised annually. Focuses mainly on scholarship and loan information for children of veterans.

Log Cabin Publishers, P.O. Box 1536-C, Allentown PA 18105. Send a self-addressed stamped envelope for a listing of helpful guides to all practical aspects of college living, choosing majors, job-hunting.

HELPFUL GROUPS

Alcoholics Anonymous World Services, P.O. Box 459, Grand Central Station, New York, NY 10163. (212) 686-1100.

A fellowship of men, women, and young adults who share the common problem of alcoholism. 42,000 local groups, listed in area phone books.

Al-Anon Family Group Headquarters, P. O. Box 862, Midtown Station, New York NY 10018. (212) 302-7240.

For relatives and friends of people with an alcoholic problem. Membership includes Alateen for members ages twelve to twenty whose lives have been adversely affected by someone else's drinking. Local groups listed in area telephone books.

National Council on Alcoholism, 12 W. 21st St., New York, NY 10010. (212) 206-6770.

Works for the prevention and control of alcoholism through programs of public and professional education, community services, speakers' bureau of recovered alcoholics and other preventive methods.

Mothers Against Drunk Driving (MADD), 669 Airport Parkway, Hurst, TX 76053. (817) 268-6233; (800) 438-6233.

Encourages citizen participation in reform of drunk driving problems. Acts as a voice of the victim(s) by speaking to the community on their behalf. Promotes educational materials, sets up local task forces, attends court hearings as watchers and offers support to victims and their families.

Students Against Driving Drunk, P.O. Box 800, Marlboro, MA 01752. (508) 481-3568.

Over 20,000 local groups, most in high schools, urge students to take a stand against drunk driving and educate their peers.

Families Anonymous, P.O. Box 528, Van Nuys, CA 91408. (818) 989-7841.

Almost 500 local groups of parents, relatives and friends concerned about substance abuse or related behavior problems in the home. Groups meet regularly, patterning themselves after AA and Al-Anon. Members assist each other in overcoming the urge to overprotect drug abusers and in improving interfamily relationships and other teen-related situations.

Toughlove, P. O. Box 1069, Doylestown PA 18901. (215) 348-7090.

A support network of over 2000 groups for parents of problem teenagers based on the premise that troubled adolescents need discipline as well as understanding and forgiveness. Members are encouraged to set minimum standards of behavior, to refuse intervention in cases of arrest and in extreme cases, to insist that the child move out, most often to another Toughlove home in the vicinity. Book, newsletter and speakers available.

National Self-Help Clearing House, Graduate School and University Center, City University of New York, 33 W. 42nd Street, New York, NY 10036. (212) 840-1259.

General clearing house of information concerning all types of self-help groups.

Birthright, 686 N. Broad, Woodbury, NJ 08096. (609) 848-1819. (800) 848-5683 from 8 a.m. to midnight, 7 days a week for referral and counseling service.

Over 400 groups operating independently throughout the country to help pregnant women find alternatives to abortion. Operates childbirth classes and parenting programs for teens and young adults; offers counselling and speakers. Can refer to specific social services for help with continuing education, shelter, clothing.

Association for Children and Adults with Learning Disabilities, 4156 Library Rd., Pittsburgh, PA 15234. (412) 341-1515.

Over 800 chapters composed of parents of children and teens with learning disabilities. Chapters educate each other and the public, help advance the cause of the learning disabled, offer speakers, information services and publications.

National Association of Anorexia Nervosa and Associated Disorders (ANAD); P.O. Box 7, Highland Park, IL 60035. (708) 831-3438.

Parents Without Partners, 8807 Colesville Rd., Silver Spring, MD 20910. (301) 588-9354.

A group for custodial and non-custodial single parents. Over 800 local groups promote family-oriented social activities, maintain speakers and activities designed to promote the acceptance and alleviate the problems of single parents and their children.

Big Brothers/Big Sisters of America, 230 N. 13th St., Philadelphia, PA 19107. (215) 567-7000.

These helping groups serve local agencies who provide children from single-parent families with adult volunteers who act as friends and companions, matched by trained workers who supervise and support the relationship. Big Brothers/Big Sisters offers regular guidance, understanding and friendship to children who have only one parent or role model.

Project Respect, P.O.Box 97, Golf, IL 60029-0097.

For an Info-Pack, a collection of information on the abstinence-based sex education program, send $3.00. For the entire package (student, teacher and parent manuals), enclose $28.50.

HOT-LINES

Child Abuse Listening Mediation, 24-hour hot-line: (800) 4-A-CHILD. For parents who feel they cannot cope with their frustrations and may be in danger of abusing their children. Listening service, referral to support organizations, other resource services.

National Runaway Switchboard, Illinois: (800) 961-4000; National: (800) 621-4000. 24-hour toll-free switchboard for runaways and the families of runaways. Provides names and addresses of shelters across the country for kids on the road. Offers to relay messages between young people and their families. Confidentiality is maintained.

Runaway Hot-Line, Texas: (800) 392-3352; National: (800) 231-6946. Formerly called Operation Peace of Mind. 24-hour national toll-free hot-line, a means for runaways to contact their parents to let them know they are safe, without having their whereabouts revealed. No attempt is made to discover location of caller, no information given to relatives other than what caller asks.

Nine-Line, 999-9999, a national hotline sponsored by Covenant House in New York City, a shelter for abused teenagers. Parents and adolescents may call the Nine-Line any time to discuss problems.

VD National Hotline, 8:00 a.m. to 8:00 p.m. (800) 227-8922; California (800) 982-5883. Information on sexually-transmitted diseases; offers referrals to clinics.

National Cocaine Hotline, 1-800-COCAINE.

Index